PENGUIN BO

On

Niccolò Machiavelli
1469–1527

Niccolò Machiavelli
On Conspiracies

TRANSLATED BY LESLIE J. WALKER, SJ
WITH REVISIONS BY BRIAN RICHARDSON

PENGUIN BOOKS — GREAT IDEAS

PENGUIN BOOKS

Published by the Penguin Group
Penguin Books Ltd, 80 Strand, London WC2R ORL, England
Penguin Group (USA) Inc., 375 Hudson Street, New York, New York 10014,
USA Penguin Group (Canada), 90 Eglinton Avenue East, Suite 700, Toronto, Ontario, Canada M4P 2Y3
(a division of Pearson Penguin Canada Inc.)
Penguin Ireland, 25 St Stephen's Green, Dublin 2, Ireland (a division of Penguin Books Ltd)
Penguin Group (Australia), 250 Camberwell Road, Camberwell, Victoria 3124, Australia
(a division of Pearson Australia Group Pty Ltd)
Penguin Books India Pvt Ltd, 11 Community Centre, Panchsheel Park,
New Delhi – 110 017, India
Penguin Group (NZ), 67 Apollo Drive, Rosedale, North Shore 0632, New Zealand
(a division of Pearson New Zealand Ltd)
Penguin Books (South Africa) (Pty) Ltd, 24 Sturdee Avenue, Rosebank, Johannesburg 2196,
South Africa

Penguin Books Ltd, Registered Offices: 80 Strand, London WC2R ORL, England

www.penguin.com

Extracts taken from *The Discourses*, first published in this edition in 1970 with an introduction
by Bernard Crick and subsequently revised and updated 1974, 1998, 2003
This selection published in Penguin Books 2010

I

ISBN: 978-0-141-19277-2

www.greenpenguin.co.uk

Penguin Books is committed to a sustainable future
for our business, our readers and our planet.
The book in your hands is made from paper
certified by the Forest Stewardship Council.

Contents

On conspiracies

Since conspiracies are of such dangerous consequence alike to princes and to private persons, I cannot well omit to discuss their nature, for it is plain that many more princes have lost their lives and their states *Introductory* in this way than by open war, because it is given to but few to make open war on a prince, whereas anyone can conspire against him. There is, on the other hand, no enterprise in which private persons can engage more dangerous or more rash than is this, for it is both difficult and extremely dangerous in all its stages. Whence it comes about that, though many conspiracies have been attempted, very few have attained the desired end. Hence, in order that princes may learn how to guard against these dangers, and that private persons may think twice before undertaking them and may learn, instead, to be content with life under the regime which fate has placed over them, I shall speak of conspiracies at length, omitting nothing of importance that is relevant either to a prince or to a private person. There is, in fact, a golden saying voiced by Cornelius Tacitus, who says that men have to respect the past but to submit to the present, and, while they should be desirous of having good princes, should put up with them of whatever sort they may turn out to be. And unquestionably those who act otherwise usually bring disaster both upon themselves and upon their country.

In starting to deal with this topic the first thing to be considered is against whom conspiracies are formed. It will be found that they are formed either against one's fatherland or against a prince. I propose here to discuss both these types, for of conspiracies formed with a view to handing over a town to the enemy besieging it or conspiracies which for one reason or another resemble this, enough has been said elsewhere.

We shall deal in the first part of this discourse with conspiracies against a prince, and shall inquire first as to *Causes* their causes, which are many. There is, however, one which is much more important than all the rest. This consists in the universal hatred a prince may evoke, for when a prince has aroused such universal hatred it is to be expected that there will be certain persons to whom he has given greater offence and that they will seek vengeance. This desire will be intensified by the universal ill will which they notice has been aroused against him. A prince, therefore, should avoid incurring these personal reproaches, and since what he has to do in order to avoid them has been discussed elsewhere I shall refrain from discussing it here: I mention it because, if he does guard against this, the mere giving of offence to individuals will evoke less hostility. The reason is, first, that one rarely comes across men so indignant at an unjust act as to endanger themselves to such an extent by seeking vengeance; and secondly, that, should they actually be inclined to do this and have the requisite power, they are restrained by the universal goodwill which they see that the prince enjoys.

Injuries may affect either a man's property, his life or

his honour. The threat of bloodshed is more dangerous than is the shedding of blood. To threaten to shed blood is, in fact, extremely dangerous: whereas to shed it is attended with no danger at all, for a dead man cannot contemplate vengeance, and those that remain alive usually leave you to do the contemplating. But a man who has been threatened and sees that he must of necessity either do something or be for it, has been turned into a real menace for the prince, as we shall cite cases presently to show.

Prescinding from the case in which action is imposed by necessity, injuries affecting a man's property or honour are the two things which give men greater offence than anything else, and against them the prince should be on his guard, for he can never so despoil anyone but that there will remain to him a knife with which to wreak vengeance. Nor can he deprive a man of his honour to such an extent that his mind will cease to be set on vengeance. And of the honours of which men may be deprived, that which imports most is a woman's honour, and, after that, contempt for a man's person. It was this that caused Pausanias to take up arms against Philip of Macedon; and this that has caused many others to take up arms against many other princes. In our day Lucio Belanti would not have been moved to conspire against Pandolfo, the tyrant of Siena, if he had not given him his daughter to wife and then taken her away again, as we shall relate in due course. The chief cause which led the Pazzi to conspire against the Medici was the inheritance of Giovanni Bonromei of which they had been deprived by the Medici's orders.

Another cause, and this a very powerful one, that makes men conspire against a prince, is the desire to liberate their fatherland of which a prince has seized possession. It was this that caused Brutus and Cassius to turn against Caesar; this that led to many other conspiracies, against Phalaris, Dionysius and against other usurpers of their country's rights. Nor can any tyrant prevail over this spirit, except by discarding his tyranny. And since one does not find tyrants doing this, one finds few who have not come to a miserable end. Hence the verse of Juvenal:

> To Pluto's realm few kings unscathed descend,
> Nor tyrants oft escape a sticky end.

The dangers involved in conspiracies, as I have said above, are considerable, and go on all the time, for in a *One-man conspiracies* conspiracy dangers crop up alike in forming the plot, in carrying it out, and as a result of its having been carried out. Plots may be formed by one conspirator, or by several. If by one person only, it cannot rightly be called a conspiracy. Rather it is a firm resolve on the part of some individual to kill the prince. Of the three dangers conspiracies entail, a one-man conspiracy lacks the first. For no danger can arise before the time for action comes, since no one else being privy to the secret, there is no danger of the plot being carried to the ears of the prince. To make a resolve of this kind lies within the competence of anybody whatsoever, be he great, small, noble or insignificant, intimate or not intimate with the prince. For anyone is allowed at some time or other to speak to the prince, and anyone who gets the chance of speaking to him, gets a chance to relieve his feelings. Pausanias, of whom we have already spoken several times, killed Philip of Macedon as he was on his way to the temple with a lot of armed men about him and his son on one side and his son-in-law on the other. The former, however, was a nobleman and an acquaintance of the prince. [But there are others.] A poor, miserable Spaniard stuck a dagger in the neck of Ferdinand, king of Spain, and, though the wound was not fatal, it shows us that a man of this type may have both the intention and the opportunity of doing such a thing. A dervish, or Turkish priest, struck at Bajazet, the father of the present Turk, with a scimitar. He did not kill him, but he certainly had the intention and the opportunity of so doing. One finds plenty of people, I think, who would like to do such things, for the intention is attended neither with penalty nor danger of any kind. Yet there are but few who actually do such things, and of those who do, there are very few, if any, who do not themselves get killed in the very act. Hence one does not find men keen on going to certain death. But let us leave these one-man plots and turn to conspiracies involving several people.

I maintain that one finds in history that all conspiracies have been made by men of standing or else by men in immediate attendance on a prince, for other people, unless they be sheer lunatics, cannot form a conspiracy; since men without power and those who are not in touch with a prince are devoid alike of any hope and of any opportunity of carrying out a conspiracy successfully. For, first of all, men without power cannot get hold of

Conspiracies formed by the weak

5

anyone who will keep faith with them, since no one can consent to do what they want under any of those prospects which induce men to take great risks, so that, once the plot has been communicated to two or three people, an informer will turn up and they are ruined. Moreover, should they actually be lucky enough to avoid informers, the carrying out of the plot will involve them in such difficulties, owing to the lack of easy access to the prince, that it will be impossible for them to escape disaster in carrying out their scheme. For, if men of standing and those who have easy access succumb to these difficulties, which will be dealt with presently, it is to be expected that in the case of these others such difficulties will be magnified without end. Consequently, since when their lives and property are not at stake, men do not entirely lose their heads, they become cautious when they recognize their weakness, and when they get sick of a prince confine themselves to cursing him, and wait for those of higher standing than they have, to avenge them. So that, should one in fact come across somebody of this kind who has attempted such a thing, one should praise his intention but not his prudence.

It would seem, then, that conspirators have all been men of standing or intimates of the prince, and, of these, those who have been moved to conspire by too many benefits are as numerous as those moved to conspire by too many injuries, as was the case with Perennis *versus* Commodus, Plautianus *versus* Severus, and Sejanus *versus* Tiberius. For to all these men their emperors had granted such wealth and so many honours and titles that there

Conspiracies formed by the strong

seemed to be nothing wanting to complete their power, save the imperial title; so, since with the lack of this they were unwilling to put up, they were moved to conspire against their prince, and their conspiracy in each case was attended with the results which their ingratitude merited.

Of similar conspiracies which have occurred in more recent times there is, however, one that met with success, that of Jacopo di Appiano against Messer Piero Gambacorti, prince of Pisa; for this Jacopo had been brought up by, reared by, and owed his reputation to, the very person whom later on he deprived of his power. There is also in our own times the conspiracy of Coppola against king Ferdinand of Aragon; the said Coppola having attained a greatness such that the only thing that seemed to him to be lacking was a kingdom, and since he made up his mind to acquire this, he lost his life. And yet, if any conspiracies against a prince, made by men of standing, ought to have succeeded it should surely have been this, since it was made by another king, so to speak, who had every convenience requisite to satisfying his desire. But that lust for domination, which blinds men, blinds them yet again in the way they set about the business: for, if they knew but how to do their evil deeds with prudence, it would be impossible for them not to succeed.

A prince, therefore, who wants to guard against conspiracies, should fear those on whom he has conferred *A warning* excessive favours more than those to whom *to princes* he has done excessive injury. For the latter lack opportunity, whereas the former abound in it, and the desire is the same in both cases; for the desire to rule is as great as, or greater than, is the desire for vengeance. Consequently princes should confer on their friends an authority of such magnitude that between it and that of the prince there remains a certain interval, and between the two a something else to be desired. Otherwise it will be a strange thing if that does not happen to them which happened to the princes we have been talking about. But to return to the lines of our discourse.

Having said that conspirators must be men of standing and have easy access to the prince, I must now discuss *The danger* the success of these, their undertaking, and *due to* inquire as to why some have succeeded and *informers* others have failed. As I have remarked above, in conspiracies there are three stages at which danger may be found to occur: at the start, while carrying them out, and afterwards. One finds that few conspiracies prove successful because it is impossible, or almost impossible, to pass through all three stages successfully. Let us begin by discussing the dangers incurred at the outset. These are the more important, I maintain, since there is need of great discretion and one must have considerable luck if, in making one's plans, the plot is not to be discovered. Plots are discovered either from information received or by conjecture. Leakage of information is due either to lack of loyalty or to lack of discretion among those to whom you communicate the plot. Lack of loyalty may easily occur, because you can only communicate your plan to those in whom you have such confidence that you think they will risk death for your sake, or else to men who are discontented with the prince. Now there may be one or two persons whom you can trust, but it is

8

impossible to find such men if you reveal your plans to many people, for the goodwill they bear you must indeed be great if the danger and the fear of punishment is not to outweigh it in their estimation. Men, too, quite frequently make mistakes about the affection another man has for them, nor can you be sure of it unless of it you have previously had experience, and to acquire experience in such a matter is a very risky business. Even should you have had experience of some other dangerous affair in which they have been loyal to you, you cannot infer from their loyalty in this case that they will be equally loyal in another which far exceeds it in dangers of all kinds. While if you judge of a person's loyalty by the degree of disaffection he has for the prince, here, too, you may easily be mistaken; for by the very fact of your having opened your mind to such a malcontent, you provide him with material with which to obtain contentment, so that, if he is to keep faith with you, either his hatred must be great or your influence over him must be very great indeed.

It thus comes about that conspiracies are frequently revealed and are crushed at the very start. Indeed, it is looked on as a marvel if a plot which has been communicated to many people, remains secret for any length of time, as was the case with that formed by Piso against Nero, and in our day with that formed by the Pazzi against Lorenzo and Juliano de' Medici, to which there were privy more than fifty persons and yet it was not discovered till it came to the point of execution.

As to discovery due to lack of discretion, this comes about when a conspiracy is spoken of without due caution and a servant or some third person gets to hear of it, as happened to the sons of Brutus who were overheard

The danger due to indiscretion discussing their plans with Tarquin's messengers by a servant who informed against them. Or it may be due to your having lightly communicated it to a lady friend or to a boy friend or to some other frivolous person, as did Dymnus, who with Philotas and others conspired against Alexander the Great, and talked of the conspiracy to Nicomachus, a boy of whom he was fond, who at once told his brother, Cebalinus, about it, and Cebalinus told it to the king.

As to discovery due to conjecture, we have an example of this in the Pisonian conspiracy formed against Nero, in

Discovery due to conjecture which Scaevinus, one of the conspirators, made his will on the day before he had to kill Nero, ordered Milichus, his freedman, to have his old and rusty dagger sharpened up, freed all his slaves and gave them money, and had bandages got ready for binding up the wounded; from which facts Milichus conjectured that there was a plot and told Nero. Scaevinus was arrested, together with Natales, another conspirator, who had been seen talking together for a long time and in secret the day before; and, as their explanations did not agree, they were forced to tell the truth; so that the conspiracy was discovered, with disastrous results for all concerned in it.

Against discovery due to such causes it is impossible so to guard as to prevent the plot being revealed, whether

The difficulty or preventing discovery owing to malice, to indiscretion or to frivolous conversation, in all cases in which the number of those who are cognizant of it exceeds three or four. For, should more than one of the conspirators be arrested, it is impossible to prevent its coming out, because two cannot possibly agree as to every detail in the explanations they give. If only one man is arrested and he be a man of resolution, he may have sufficient strength of mind to be silent about his fellow conspirators. It is essential, however, that the other conspirators have no less courage than he has in standing their ground and not running away, for the conspiracy will be revealed by either party in which courage is lacking, whether by the man who has been arrested or those who are still at large.

There is, indeed, a rare case given by Titus Livy, namely, the conspiracy formed against Hieronymus, king of Syracuse, in which, when Theodotus, one of the conspirators, was arrested, he showed great virtue in concealing all the other conspirators, and accused the king's own friends; and the other conspirators, on their part, had such confidence in Theodotus's virtue, that not one of them left Syracuse or showed any other sign of fear.

These, then, are the dangers to which a conspiracy is exposed in the course of its formation before the time comes for it to be carried out; and, if *Precautions against discovery* they are to be avoided, these are the remedies. The first, the safest and, to tell the truth, the only one, is not to allow the conspirators time to give information against you, and to tell them of your plan only when you are ready to act, and not before. Those who have so acted, at any rate escape the dangers involved in contriving the plot, and more often than not, the others also. All of them, in fact, have been successful, and any prudent man should find it possible to conduct things in this fashion. I shall cite two cases, and leave it at that.

Nelematus, being unable to stand the tyranny of Aristotimus, tyrant of Epirus, collected in his house many of his relations and friends, and exhorted them to set their country free. Some of them asked for time to consider the matter and to put their affairs in order. Whereupon Nelematus told his servants to lock the doors of the house, and to those whom he had called together said: 'Either you swear to go and do the deed now, or I shall hand you all over as prisoners to Aristotimus.' These words got them going; they took the oath, and, having set out without delay, they successfully carried out Nelematus's instructions. When one of the Magi by subterfuge got possession of the Persian throne, and Otanes, one of the leading men in the kingdom, heard of it and discovered the fraud, he conferred with six other leading men in the state, and told them that it was for them to rid the kingdom of the tyranny of this Magus. When one of them asked for time, Darius, one of the six who had been called together by Otanes, got up and said: 'Either we go at once and put this business through, or I shall go and lay information against the lot of you.' So with one accord they got up, and succeeded in carrying out their plan before anyone had time to repent. Similar to these two cases also was the method the Aetolians adopted in order to kill Nabis, the Spartan tyrant; for they commissioned their fellow-citizen, Alexamenes, to go with thirty horse and two hundred foot ostensibly to the assistance of Nabis, communicated the secret only to Alexamenes, and told the rest to obey him on each and every point under pain of banishment. So Alexamenes went to Sparta and never mentioned the commission entrusted to him till he was ready to carry it out; with the result that he succeeded in killing Nabis. These folk, then, by adopting these methods, have avoided the dangers which attend the planning of a conspiracy; and those who follow their example will always avoid them.

That anyone can do as they did, I propose now to prove by citing the case of Piso, of whom mention has already been made. Piso was a man of very high standing and great repute, and was intimate with Nero, who had considerable confidence in him. Nero used frequently to dine with him in his gardens. Piso, therefore, could have made friends with men who in mentality, courage and inclination were of the right kind to carry out such a scheme, for to a man of standing this is quite an easy matter; and while Nero was in his gardens, he could have told them of the business and with suitable words got them to do what there would have been no time for them to refuse and what could not but have succeeded. Hence if we inquire into conspiracies in general, but few will be found that could not have been carried out in the same way. Ordinarily, however, men pay but little attention to the affairs of the world and so make frequently the gravest blunders, especially in matters which lie outside the ordinary run of things, as this does.

A plot, then, should never be divulged unless one is driven to it and it is ripe for execution, and if you, perforce, have to divulge it, it should be told to but one other

Their practicability

person, and this a man of whom you have had very considerable experience, or else one who is actuated by the

same motives as you are. To find such a man is far easier than to find several, and for this very reason is less dangerous. Moreover, should you, in fact, make a mistake, you have here a chance of protecting yourself, which is not the case where many conspirators are involved. For I have heard a wise man say that you can talk about anything to one person alone, since, unless you allow yourself to be persuaded to commit yourself in writing, one man's 'yes' will be worth just as much as the other man's 'no'. And against writing anything down everybody should be on his guard as against a rock, for nothing is more likely to convict you than is your own handwriting. Plautianus, having made up his mind to kill the emperor, Severus, and his son, Antoninus, entrusted the secret to Saturninus, the tribune, who wanted to inform against him instead of doing what he wished, but was afraid that, when he brought the charge, more credence might be given to Plautianus than to himself. So he asked for something in writing that might serve as evidence of the commission entrusted to him. Blinded by ambition, Plautianus gave it him, with the result that the tribune brought the accusation and he was convicted. Yet without this commitment in writing and certain other evidence against him, Plautianus would have got the better of him, so brazen was he in denying the charge. There is then some chance of getting off when a charge is brought by but one person provided you cannot be convicted by a written document or other evidence telling against you, which one should take care not to provide.

In the Pisonian conspiracy there was a woman called Epicharis, who had formerly been Nero's mistress. Since she thought it would help to get a captain of some triremes which served as Nero's guard to join the conspirators, she told him of the plot, but not who the conspirators were. Subsequently, when the captain broke his word and charged her with it to Nero, Epicharis denied the charge with such vehemence that Nero could not make up his mind and let her off. There are, then, in communicating a plot to a single other person two dangers: the first is that he may accuse you of his own accord; and the second is that he may get arrested on suspicion or because there is some evidence against him, and accuse you when convicted and constrained by torture to do so. In both these cases the danger is not irremediable; for in the first case you can deny the charge and allege that he made it because he hated you; and in the second you can deny it, alleging that under force he has been compelled to tell a lie.

The wisest thing, therefore, is not to tell anybody what you are about, but to act in accordance with the examples given above; or, if you have to tell somebody, not to tell more than one, in which case, though the danger will be somewhat greater, it will not be so great as if you had told it to many. The case is somewhat the same when necessity constrains you to do that to a prince which you see that the prince is about to do to you, for your need is then so great that it does not give you time to think of precautions. A necessity of this kind almost always leads to the end desired; and, to prove it, I propose to give just two examples.

Unpremeditated assassination

Among the chief friends and intimates which the emperor, Commodus, had, were Laetus and Eclectus, who were in charge of his praetorian troops, and for one of his principal concubines or lady friends he had Marcia; and because they sometimes reproached him for sullying alike his person and his imperial position by his behaviour, he decided to put them to death, and made out a list on which he wrote the names of Marcia, Laetus and Eclectus, and several others whom he proposed on the following night to put to death. This list he put under the pillow of his bed. Having gone to wash himself, a favourite little boy of his was romping about the room and on the bed when he came across the list, and, having gone outside with it in his hand, met Marcia, who took it from him, and, having read it and noted its contents, sent at once for Laetus and Eclectus. All three of them, realizing the danger in which they stood, decided to forestall it; so, without wasting any unnecessary time, they killed Commodus the following night.

Again, the emperor Antoninus Caracalla, when with his army in Mesopotamia, had as his prefect Macrinus, who was more of a civilian than a soldier; and, as is usually the case with princes who are not good, he was for ever afraid that others should not act towards him as he thought he deserved. So Antoninus wrote to Maternianus, a friend of his in Rome, to request him to inquire of the astrologers whether anybody was aspiring to become emperor, and to advise him accordingly. Maternianus, therefore, wrote him that Macrinus was the man who had this idea in mind, but the letter fell into the hands of Macrinus before it got to the emperor, and, in consequence, Macrinus saw that it was necessary either to kill him before a further letter came from Rome, or to be killed; so he instructed Martialis, a centurion who was devoted to him and whose brother Antoninus had killed a few days before, to assassinate the emperor, a commission which he carried out successfully.

Hence we see that when necessity becomes so urgent that it leaves no time for delay, it produces much the same effect as does the method adopted by Nelematus of Epirus, which I have described above. We see, too, that what I have said almost at the beginning of this discourse also holds good, namely, that threats do more harm to princes and are more likely to result in conspiracies than the actual infliction of injuries. Against threats, therefore, a prince should be on his guard; for either he should make a fuss of men or should make sure they will do him no harm, but in no case should he put them in such a position that the only courses which appear open to them are either to get killed or to kill somebody else.

As to the dangers which occur during the carrying out of a plot, these are due either to a change of plan, or to

Dangers arising from a change of plan

lack of courage on the part of the person who is to carry it out, or to the operative's making some mistake owing to carelessness, or to failure to complete the job in that there remain alive some of those who were to have been killed. I would here point out, therefore, that nothing so perturbs and interferes with anything undertaken by men as does their having suddenly and without due notice to change their plan and to give up that laid down at the start. And, if such a change of plan

anywhere gives rise to disorder, it is in military operations and in affairs such as those of which we are speaking; because in a business of this kind what it is essential
to do first and foremost is to get clearly into the heads of
those concerned the part which each of them has to play,
and, if men have for several days been picturing to themselves a certain course of action and a certain plan, and
this is suddenly changed, it is impossible but that it should
throw everything out of gear and spoil the whole scheme.
So that it is much better to carry out the original plan,
even if one sees in it certain inconveniences, than it is to
cancel it and thereby to involve oneself in a host of inconveniences. This applies to cases in which there is no time
to draw up a new plan, for, if there is time, a man can
arrange matters as he pleases.

The conspiracy of the Pazzi against Lorenzo and
Giuliano de' Medici is familiar to all. According to the plan
that had been given out, they were to be invited to dinner
with the Cardinal of St George, and at the dinner were to
be assassinated. Those who were to kill them, those who
were to seize the palace and those who were to run about
the city calling on the people to free themselves, had all
been detailed. It happened that, when the Pazzi, the
Medici and the Cardinal were attending a solemn function in the cathedral church of Florence, it became
known that Giuliano was not going to dine with them
that day; so the conspirators got together and decided
that what they had been going to do in the house of the
Medici should be done in the church. This upset the
whole plan, for Giovambatista da Montesecco declined
to take part in the murder, since he was not going to do

it in church, he said. So they had to find new operatives and to redistribute the parts assigned, and, since there was no time for them to get clear as to their parts, they made such blunders in carrying it out that they were overcome.

Irresolution on the part of operatives in doing their job, is due either to human respect or to personal cow-

Failure due to irresolution

ardice. Such is the majesty and the respect inspired by the presence of a prince that it may easily damp the resolution of an operative or terrify him. When Marius was taken prisoner by the Minturnians a slave was sent to kill him, but, so overawed was he by the presence of such a man and by the recollection of what his name stood for, that he lost courage and hadn't the strength to kill him. If, then, such power appertains to a man who is chained up in prison and overwhelmed with misfortune, how much greater must be that of a prince who is not thus encumbered, but is there in his majesty, wearing his robes and decorations, surrounded by pomp and by his courtiers. Such pomp as this may well affright you, or again the graciousness of his welcome may soften you. Certain persons were conspiring against Sitalces, king of Thrace, had settled the day on which the deed was to be done, and had got to the place assigned at which the prince then was; yet none of them ventured to attack him, so that at length they went away without trying to do anything and without quite knowing what had prevented them, each laying the blame on the other. They made the same mistake more than once, so that in the end the conspiracy was discovered and they were punished for a crime which they could have committed but were reluctant to commit. Two of his brothers conspired against Alfonso, Duke of Ferrara, and used as an intermediary Giannes, a priest and a cantor in the duke's employ. Several times at their request he got the duke to meet them, so that it lay in their power to kill him; in spite of which not one of them dared to do it, so that, the plot being discovered, they suffered the penalty of their wickedness and their want of prudence. Such negligence could not have been due to anything except their being frightened by the presence of the prince or humbled by some gracious act of his.

Inconveniences in the carrying out of a conspiracy are due to mistakes caused either by lack of prudence or by

Failure due to perturbation of mind

lack of courage, for both these two things may befall you and cause you such confusion of mind that you say and do what you oughtn't to say or do. That men do get thus overwhelmed and confused cannot be better illustrated than by what Titus Livy tells us of Alexamenes, the Aetolian, who had made up his mind to kill Nabis the Spartan, of whom we have already spoken. When the time came to do it, he explained to his men what it was they had to do, and, says Livy, 'pulled himself together, for his mind had become confused by thinking of so great a matter'. It is, indeed, impossible, that any man, even though he be strongminded, familiar with death and accustomed to using the sword, should not become confused. Hence men should be chosen who have had experience in doing such deeds, and one should entrust them to no one else, brave as he may be thought to be. For when it comes to doing big things of which a man has had no previous experience, no one can say for certain what will happen. This confusion, for instance, might be such as to cause you to let the weapon fall from your hand, or to let slip some word which would have precisely the same effect. Lucilla, the sister of Commodus, arranged with Quintianus to kill him. Quintianus lay in wait for Commodus at the entrance to the amphitheatre, and, going up to him with a naked dagger, greeted him with the words: 'The senate sends you this!', words which led to his being arrested before he had lowered his arm to strike. Messer Antonio de Volterra was deputed, as we have already said, to kill Lorenzo de' Medici. On coming up to him he said: 'Ah, traitor!', an exclamation which saved Lorenzo's life and ruined the conspiracy.

It is not easy to do the thing perfectly when a conspiracy is directed against one ruler, for the reasons alleged, and still less is it easy to do it perfectly when a conspiracy is directed against two. On the contrary, it is so difficult that it is almost impossible for the conspiracy to succeed. For it is almost impossible to do similar actions in different places at one and the same time, and you cannot perform them at different times if you do not want one to spoil the other. Hence, if to conspire against one prince is a doubtful, dangerous and imprudent undertaking, to conspire against two is altogether foolish and frivolous. Were it not for my respect for the historian I should never have thought that what Herodian says of Plautianus were possible, namely, that he should have commissioned the same person, Saturninus the centurion, to kill both Severus and Antoninus who

Conspiracies directed against more than one prince

21

dwelt in different places, for the thing is so utterly unreasonable that nothing short of his authority would make me believe it.

Certain Athenian youths conspired against Diocles and Hippias, tyrants ruling in Athens. They killed Diocles, but Hippias escaped and avenged him. Chion and Leonides of Heraclea, disciples of Plato, conspired against the tyrants, Clearchus and Satyrus. They killed Clearchus, but Satyrus remained alive to avenge him. The Pazzi, whom we have mentioned more than once, only succeeded in killing Giuliano. Hence no one should engage in conspiracies against more than one ruler since he will do not good either to himself or to his country or to anybody at all. On the contrary, those who survive, will become more insupportable and more bitter, as Florence, Athens and Heraclea, to which I have already alluded, found out. True, the conspiracy which Pelopidas formed for the liberation of Thebes, his fatherland, involved all these difficulties, and yet was successful; for Pelopidas conspired not only against two tyrants, but against ten, and not only was he an outsider to whom access to the tyrants presented a difficulty, but he was a rebel. None the less, he was able to get into Thebes, to kill the tyrants and to liberate his country. Actually, however, it was with the assistance of Charon, counsellor to the tyrants, that he did all this, for it was through him that he gained easy access to do the deed. Nor should anyone nevertheless emulate his example; for it was an impossible undertaking and a marvellous thing that it succeeded. It was also, as all writers are agreed who have mentioned it, a rare and almost unparalleled thing.

The carrying out of a plot may be ruined by a false impression or by an unforeseen accident which occurs in the course of it. On the very morning on which Brutus and the other conspirators had decided to kill Caesar, it happened that he held a long conversation with Gaius Pompilius Lenas, who was one of the conspirators, and when the others saw him talking for so long, they wondered whether the said Pompilius was not telling Caesar of the conspiracy, and were on the point of killing him there and then, without waiting for him to come into the senate. They would, indeed, have done this, had the argument not come to an end and had they not then been reassured when they saw Caesar gave no sign of unusual emotion. False impressions of this kind should be taken into account and due attention be paid to them, if one would be prudent; the more so in that it is easy to get such false impressions. For, when a man has a bad conscience, he readily believes that people are talking about him, and a remark which is irrelevant may disturb your equanimity and make you think that it has bearing on your business, and this causes you either to give the conspiracy away by running off, or to muddle it by acting before the proper time. And the more there are who are in the know, the more likely is this to happen.

Failure due to false impressions

As to accidents, since they cannot be foreseen, the only thing one can do is to give examples showing how cautious men ought to be in regard to them. Lucio Belanti of Siena, of whom mention has already been made, was so indignant with Pandolfo, who had taken away the daughter he had previously given him in marriage, that he decided to kill him, and chose the occasion as follows. Pandolfo used to go daily to visit a sick relative, and, in

Failure due to unforeseen accidents

doing so, passed by Lucio's house. Lucio, having noticed this, arranged for his conspirators to be ready in his house to kill Pandolfo as he was going by. He placed them inside the doorway with their arms, and stationed one of them at the window ready to give the signal when Pandolfo was to pass by the doorway, whereupon they were at once to issue forth. It so happened that, when Pandolfo came along and the signal had been given, Pandolfo met a friend who stopped him, and some of those who were with him went on ahead, saw what was happening, heard the clatter of arms and so discovered the trap; with the result that Pandolfo escaped and Lucio and his accomplices had to fly from Siena. Thus this accidental meeting interfered with the business in hand and caused Lucio's scheme to end in disaster. Since accidents, such as these, are of rare occurrence, it is impossible to prescribe any remedy. What one must do is to consider everything that is likely to happen, and to provide accordingly.

It remains now for us to discuss the dangers that may occur after a conspiracy has been successfully carried out.

Dangers subsequent to a conspiracy

There is but one. It is that someone may be left alive who will avenge the death of the prince. There may, for instance, remain brothers or sons or other supporters to whom the principality was expected to come. Survival of those who may wreak vengeance may be due either to your negligence or to the causes mentioned above. Thus, when Giovanni Andrea da Lampognano and his accomplices had killed the Duke of Milan, there remained one of his sons and two of his brothers, who in due course came to avenge his death. In cases such as these the conspirators have an excuse, for there is nothing they can do about it; but when it is owing to lack of prudence or to their negligence that someone is left alive, they have in that case no excuse. Some conspirators who were citizens of Forli, killed Count Girolamo, their Lord, and took prisoner his wife and his children, who were little ones. It seemed to them, however, that their lives would scarce be safe unless they could get hold of the citadel, which its governor declined to hand over. So Mistress Catherine, as the countess was called, promised the conspirators that, if they would let her go to the citadel, she would arrange for it to be handed over to them. Meanwhile they were to keep her children as hostages. On this understanding the conspirators let her go to the citadel, from the walls of which, when she got inside, she reproached them with killing her husband and threatened them with vengeance in every shape and form. And to convince them that she did not mind about her children she exposed her sexual parts to them and said she was still capable of bearing more. The conspirators, dumbfounded, realized their mistake too late, and paid the penalty for their lack of prudence by suffering perpetual banishment.

But of all the dangers that may ensue after a successful conspiracy there is none more inevitable or more to be dreaded than when the people are well disposed to the prince you have killed; for in such a case, since there is no remedy to which the conspirators can have recourse, there is no chance of their ever obtaining security. Caesar is a case in point, for he was avenged by the people of Rome who were friendlily disposed towards him; and of the conspirators, after they had been driven out of Rome, one and all were killed at various times and in various places.

Conspiracies against one's country are less dangerous to those who take part in them than are conspiracies against princes, since fewer dangers occur in the planning of them than in the latter case; in carrying them out they are the same; and afterwards there are none. There are not many dangers in planning the conspiracy because a citizen can scheme to obtain power without revealing his mind or his plan to anybody else, and, if his schemes are not interfered with, success will attend his undertaking; while if they should be interfered with by some law or other, he must bide his time and look for some other opening. This applies to a republic which is to some extent corrupt, for, since in one that is not corrupt no starting on evil courses there finds a place, no citizen is likely to harbour such thoughts. There are, then, all manner of ways and means of which citizens who aspire to a principality can avail themselves without running any risk of getting into trouble, alike because a republic is slower to take action than is a prince, is less suspicious, and for this reason less cautious, and because it has more respect for citizens of standing, and, in consequence, the latter are more daring and more inclined to act contrary to its interests. Everybody has read Sallust's account of the conspiracy of Catiline, and is aware that Catiline not only remained in Rome after the conspiracy was discovered, but attended the senate, where he made opprobrious

Conspiracies against one's country

remarks about the senate and about the consuls, so great was the respect which this city had for its citizens. Nor, when he had left Rome and was already in touch with the armies, would Lentulus and others have been arrested if they had not had in their possession letters in their own hand which plainly showed their complicity.

Again, when Hanno, one of the leading citizens in Carthage, who hoped to set up a tyranny, had arranged to poison the whole senate at the marriage-feast of one of his daughters, and afterwards to make himself prince, all the senate did, when it got to hear of the business, was to pass a law restricting the amount to be spent on banquets and marriages, so great was the respect they had for a man in his position.

On the other hand, it may well be that in carrying out a conspiracy against one's country there is more difficulty and the dangers are greater, for in a conspiracy aimed at so many people your own forces will scarce suffice; and not everybody has an army at his disposal, as had Caesar, Agathocles, Cleomenes and such-like, who have at one stroke subjugated their country by means of the forces they commanded. For to such folk the way is easy enough and safe enough; but others who have not such forces at their disposal, must give effect to their designs either by means of deceit and artifice or with the help of foreign troops. The use of deceit and artifice is illustrated in the case of Pisistratus, the Athenian, who by his victory over the Megarians gained favour with the people. One morning he appeared in public, wounded, said that the nobility out of envy had attacked him, and asked that he might go about with an armed force for the protection of his person. This being authorized, he had no difficulty in arrogating to himself such great power that he became tyrant of Athens. Pandolfo Petrucci, on his return to Siena with other exiles, was given command of the guard in the Piazza, a routine business which others had refused; yet this armed force in course of time acquired for him such repute that he became before long a prince. Many others have adopted other devices and other methods and in course of time and without danger have achieved their aim.

Those who have conspired to get control of their country by means of their own forces or with foreign armies have met with varied success according as fortune has favoured them or not. Catiline, whom we mentioned above, perished in the attempt. Hanno, of whom also we made mention, having failed to succeed by using poison, armed several thousands of his partisans, and both he and they were slain. Some of the principal citizens of Thebes called in a Spartan army to help them, and set up a tyranny in that city. If, then, we inquire into all the conspiracies men have made against their country, it will be found that none of them, or but few, have been suppressed while the plot was being contrived, but that all of them have either succeeded or been ruined when it came to carrying them out. Nor, when successful, do they entail any subsequent dangers other than those which pertain to a principality by its very nature. For, given that a man has become a tyrant, he is faced with the dangers which tyranny naturally and normally involves, and to avert them has no remedies other than those that we have already discussed.

This is all that needs to be said about conspiracies, and if I have taken account of those in which the sword and

The use of poison

not poison has been used, it is because they are all of one and the same pattern. It is true that the use of poison is more dangerous owing to its being more uncertain, for not everybody has the commodity, so that those who have it must needs be consulted and the necessity of consulting others means danger to yourself. Again, for a variety of reasons, a poisoned drink may not prove fatal, as those discovered who were to kill Commodus, for, on his throwing up the poison they had given him, they were forced to strangle him if they wanted him to die.

There is nothing, then, more inimical to princes than a conspiracy. For, when a conspiracy is formed against

Tactics to be used in suppressing a conspiracy

them, either they get killed or they incur infamy; since, if it succeeds, they die, and if it is discovered and they kill the conspirators, the conspiracy is apt to be regarded as a device on the part of the prince whereby to cloak his avarice and his cruelty *vis-à-vis* the lives and property of those he has put to death. I must not, therefore, neglect to warn that prince or that republic who knows that a conspiracy has been planned, to endeavour to discover its precise character before they take punitive action, and to compare carefully the strength and standing of the conspirators with their own; and, should they find it large and powerful, to take no notice of it until they have at their disposal enough forces to crush it. To act otherwise is but to court disaster. Hence they should practise dissimulation as best they can, lest the conspirators, finding themselves discovered, be driven of necessity to take immediate action regardless of the result.

The Romans afford us an example of this. Two legions of soldiers were left to guard Capua against the Samnites, as we have pointed out elsewhere. Those who were in command of these legions conspired together to reduce the Capuans to subjection. When this came to be known in Rome, Rutilus, a new consul, was commissioned to look into the matter. To keep the conspirators quiet, he made public the senate confirmation of the Capuan legions' lodging quarters. The troops believed this, and, since there seemed to them to be plenty of time to carry out their plan, they made no attempt to hurry things. So matters stood until they came to realize that the consul had separated one legion from the other, which caused them to grow suspicious, to come out into the open and to give orders for their scheme to be put into execution. Nor can there be a better example than this from whichever point of view we look at it, for we see how slow men are to act when they think they have time, and how quick to act when the need becomes urgent. Nor yet can a prince or a republic that wants to postpone the discovery of a conspiracy in its own interests do better than artfully to provide the conspirators with an opportunity at some future date, so that, while they await it in the belief that there is no hurry, that prince or that republic may have time to arrange for their punishment.

Those who have acted otherwise have but hastened their own downfall, as the Duke of Athens did, and Guglielmo de' Pazzi. When the duke became tyrant of Florence and heard that a conspiracy had been formed against him, he had one of the conspirators arrested but did not inquire further into the matter, with the result that the rest at once flew to arms and deprived him of the government. When Guglielmo was commissioner in the Val di Chiana in 1501 and learned that a conspiracy in favour of the Virelli had been formed in Arezzo whereby the Florentines were to be deprived of that town, he went at once to that city, and without considering either the strength of the conspirators or his own and without having any forces in readiness, on the advice of the bishop, his son, he had one of the conspirators arrested. After the arrest, the remaining conspirators at once took up arms, took the town from the Florentines and Guglielmo became a prisoner instead of a commissioner.

But when conspiracies are weak they both can, and ought, to be suppressed without further ado. Nor should either of the two following expedients be adopted, though one is almost the exact opposite of the other. One was used by the aforesaid Duke of Athens, who to show that he believed the Florentines to be well disposed towards him, put to death a man who had told him of a conspiracy. The other was adopted by Dion, the Syracusan, who, to discover the intentions of someone of whom he was suspicious, allowed Callippus, whom he trusted, to pretend to be forming a conspiracy. Both these expedients led to disaster, for the first discouraged informers and encouraged would-be conspirators, and the second made it an easy matter to compass Dion's death by means of the very conspiracy of which he was the real head, as he learned by experience, for Callippus was now able without further ado to plot against Dion, and he plotted so well that he deprived him both of his state and of his life.

The army, its discipline
and component parts

How far the Discipline of Troops in our Day falls
short of that maintained in Days gone by

The most important battle ever fought by the Romans in any war with another nation was the battle they fought with the Latin peoples in the consulate of Torquatus and Decius. For everything shows that, just as the Latins by losing became a subject people, so the Romans would have become a subject people, had they not won. This is the view held by Titus Livy, for in all respects the two armies were alike in discipline, virtue, truculence and in numbers; the only difference was that the commanders of the Roman army had more virtuosity than those of the Latin army.

One notes, too, how in the conduct of this battle there occurred two unprecedented incidents of which there have been but few examples since; namely, to strengthen the resolution of the soldiers and to make them obey orders, of the two consuls one killed himself and the other killed his son. The parity which Titus Livy says held between the two armies was due to their having for a long time waged war together, and consisted in their having the same language, the same discipline, and the same kind of arms, for in drawing up troops for battle they used the same formation, and both units and officers bore the same names. It was essential, therefore, since both in strength and in *virtù* they were equal, that something extraordinary should take place whereby to strengthen the ardour and truculence of the one rather than the other, for, as we have remarked on other occasions, it is on determination that victory depends, since, so long as it lasts in the breasts of those who are fighting, an army will never turn tail. And in order that it might last longer in the breasts of the Romans than with the Latins it came about, owing partly to chance and partly to the virtue of the consuls, that Torquatus had to kill his son and Decius to kill himself.

When pointing out this parity in strength Titus Livy describes in detail how the Romans drew up their armies and how they disposed them for battle. He has done this at considerable length, so I shall not repeat it all, but shall discuss the points which I deem worthy of note, points which are ignored by all present-day commanders, with the result that there is a grave lack of proper order alike in drawing up armies and in battle. From Livy we gather that in the Roman army there were three main divisions for which the Tuscan term three 'ranks' may be used. They called the first *Hastati*, the second *Principes*, the third *Triarii*. Each had its own cavalry attached. In drawing them up for battle, they put the *Hastati* in front; in the second place, immediately behind the *Hastati*, they put the *Principes*; in the third, all covering precisely the same space, they placed the *Triarii*. The cavalry pertaining to each of these divisions they put on the right and on the left of the three formations. These mounted troops, on account of their formation and their position, were called *alae*, because they looked like two wings attached to the body. They drew up the first rank, consisting of the *Hastati* who were in front, in close formation, so that they might thrust forward and hold up the enemy. The second rank, consisting of *Principes*, since they were not to be engaged at the outset, but were to come to the aid of the first should they be beaten or hard pressed, they did not draw up in such close formation, but kept their lines thinner so that this rank could receive the first rank, without disturbing its formation, should the latter be overcome by the enemy and have to fall back. The third rank consisting of *Triarii*, were drawn up in yet thinner lines than the second, so as to receive the two first ranks, comprising *Principes* and *Hastati*, should need arise. When their ranks had thus been drawn up in this formation, they went into battle; and, should the *Hastati* be forced back or defeated, they fell straight back upon the thinner ranks of the *Principes*, and the two ranks, thus united to form one compact body, resumed the fight. Should these ranks be beaten and forced to retreat, they retired upon the thinner ranks of the *Triarii*, and all three ranks, together forming one body, renewed the fight. But should they be overcome, the day was lost, since they had no further chance to reform. Wherefore, since every time this last rank of *Triarii* became engaged, it meant danger to the army, there arose the proverb: 'It all depends on the *Triarii*', or, as we say in the Tuscan idiom: 'We have played the last stake'.

As generals in our days have abandoned all other traditions and pay no attention to any point in ancient military discipline, so they have abandoned it in regard to this point, which is of no small importance. For where an army is so drawn up as to be able to re-form three times during a battle, to lose the day luck must go against it three times and the valour of those attacking it must be sufficient to beat it three times over. But an army that can withstand but one attack, as is the case with all Christian armies, may easily lose, for, if it become in any way disorganized or its valour be but indifferent, its chance of victory goes. The inability of our armies thrice to re-form is due to their having dropped the custom of receiving one rank into the other. This in turn is due to there being in present-day battle-formations one of two defects: either they station their ranks one alongside the other, and make their formations broad in extent but thin in the line of attack, which makes them weaker owing to their lack of depth; or when, to make them stronger, they actually draw up the ranks in Roman fashion, then, since no arrangement is made for the first to be received by the second, when the first is routed, all get mixed up together and defeat themselves. For if the rank in front gets the worst of it, it collides with the second; and, if the second wants to advance, it is impeded by the first. Hence when the first falls back on the second, and the second on the third, so much confusion arises that the whole army is frequently ruined should the least misadventure befall.

At the battle of Ravenna, in which Monsieur de Foix who commanded the armies of France was killed – a well-fought battle as things go today – both the Spanish and the French armies were drawn up in one of the ways just described, i.e. each of the two armies advanced with all its troops drawn up shoulder to shoulder so that both presented but a single front which was much greater in extent than it was in depth. This is always their procedure when they are operating on a large plain such as they had at Ravenna; for, realizing the disorder a retreat causes when troops are arranged in files, they avoid this, when they can, by making their front broad, as has been said. But should the available space be narrow they put up with the aforesaid bad arrangement without providing any remedy. And in the same bad formation they ride through the enemy's country, whether to loot it or to perform any other military manoeuvre.

Again, at San Regolo in the territory of Pisa, as also at other places in which the Florentines were routed by the Pisans during the war which took place between the Florentines and that city owing to its having rebelled after Charles, king of France, passed through Italy, the disaster was entirely due to the allied cavalry which, being in front and having been repulsed by the enemy, fell back on the Florentine infantry and broke it up, so that the rest of the troops all turned tail. Messer Ciriaco dal Borgo, once a captain of Florentine infantry, has also often stated in my presence that he had never been routed except by the cavalry of his allies. The Swiss, who are masters of modern warfare, when fighting on the French side, make it their first care to station themselves on the flanks, so that, should the allied cavalry be driven back, it will not clash with them. Yet, though such things are both easy to understand and very easy to carry out, none the less there has not appeared as yet any of our contemporary generals who has adopted the ancient formations and emended the modern ones. And though they may again have the threefold army formation, called respectively the vanguard, the main body and the rearguard, it serves no purpose other than that of disposing men in billets. Moreover, when they make use of it, as was said above, it rarely happens that the self-same fortune does not befall all these bodies.

Since many, to cover their ignorance, assert that the destructive power of artillery does not in these days permit the use of many ancient practices, I propose to discuss this question in the following chapter, and to inquire whether artillery renders it impossible to display the valour of days gone by.

In what Esteem Artillery should be held by Armies at the Present Time, and whether the Opinion universally held in its Regard is Sound

When in addition to what I have just written, I consider how many open battles which in our time the French call 'days' and the Italians call 'feats of arms', were fought by the Romans at different times, there comes to my mind the common opinion so many hold, an opinion which would have it that, had there been artillery in those days, it would not have been possible for the Romans to have conquered provinces and to have made peoples become their tributaries so easily as they did; nor would they have been able in any way to make such bold acquisitions. They allege, too, that the use of these destructive weapons prevents men from employing and displaying their virtue as they used to do of old. And as a third point they add that it is more difficult than it was then to come to an engagement, and that it is impossible to keep to the ancient usages. In fact, war before long will be reduced to the question of artillery.

I do not think it beside the point to discuss whether this view is sound, or to inquire whether artillery has increased or has lessened the strength of armies, and whether it has deprived good generals of, or has provided them with, an opportunity for acting 'virtuously'. So let me begin by dealing with the first of these claims, namely, that Roman armies of old would not have made the acquisitions they did make, if in those days there had been artillery.

In reply to this I would point out that wars are either offensive or defensive. Hence we must first ask to which of these two kinds of warfare artillery is the more useful or the more dangerous. Though there is something to be said for either view, yet I am convinced that artillery is incomparably more harmful to defenders than to those who attack. The reason why I say this is that the defenders are either in a walled town or are encamped behind a stockade. If they are within a walled town, either it is small, as are most fortresses, or it is large. In the first case, it is all up with the defenders, for the force of artillery is such that no wall can stand it, not even the thickest, for more than a few days. Hence if those within have not a goodly space into which to retire and dig trenches and build ramparts they are doomed. Nor can they withstand the attack of an enemy determined to force his way through a gap in the walls, even if they have artillery to help them, for it is an accepted maxim that against a heavy massed attack artillery is powerless. For this reason the defending of towns against the fury of ultramontane attacks has not been successful but against the assaults of Italians they have been highly successful, for the latter do not attack *en masse* but in detachments, a form of attack for which much the best name is skirmishing. To advance thus coolly in such weak formation towards a breach in the walls where there is artillery, is to advance to certain death, and against such attacks artillery is of service. But when the attackers form a dense mass and come on one after the other to a breach in the walls, they get through anywhere unless held up by trenches and ramparts. Artillery will not hold them, for, though some get killed, there will not be so many killed as to prevent a victory.

That this is so is shown by the many towns stormed by the ultramontanes in Italy, and especially by that of Brescia. For when this town rebelled against the French who still held the citadel on behalf of the king of France, in order to prevent raids being made on the town from the citadel, the Venetians fortified the whole of the street leading down from the citadel to the city with artillery, placing it both in front and on the flanks and in any other convenient place. But of this Monsieur de Foix made no account. On the contrary, with a squadron of his cavalry, who dismounted, he got right through the artillery and took the city; nor do we hear that the artillery caused him any appreciable loss. So that the defenders of a small town, as we have said, when they find their walls laid low and have no space into which to retire behind ramparts and in trenches, but have to rely on their artillery, are speedily undone.

If you are defending a large town where you have all you need for a withdrawal, artillery is still of far greater use to those who are outside than to those who are within. First, because, if artillery is to do any damage to those who are outside, you must needs raise it above the level of the ground, for, if on the level, every little trench the enemy digs and every rampart he puts up will afford him security, and you can do him no harm. So much so that, having raised your artillery and dragged it into some recess in the walls or having in some other way elevated it above the ground, you will then meet with two difficulties. First, you cannot bring into action artillery of the same size and power as those outside can avail themselves of, since in a small space it is impossible to manipulate large pieces. Secondly, should you succeed in getting it there, you will not be able to construct reliable and safe ramparts whereby to protect the said artillery, which can be done quite easily outside, on *terra firma*, where there are all the conveniences and as much space as anyone can want. Hence it is impossible for the defenders of a town to have their artillery in high positions when those who are outside have enough artillery and that of a powerful kind; and if they are driven to place it in a low position, it is in large part useless, as has been said. Consequently, the defence of a city has to be carried on by hand-to-hand fighting, as was done of old, supported by artillery of very light calibre. Wherefore, though some slight benefit may accrue from this light artillery, it brings with it a disadvantage which counterbalances the advantage due to artillery, because, owing to the heavy artillery, the walls of towns are demolished and lie flat, buried, as it were, in ditches, so that, when it comes to hand-to-hand fighting, the defenders have a worse time of it than they had before, since their walls have been battered down or their trenches filled up. These engines of war, therefore, as was said above, are of more use to the besiegers of towns than they are to the besieged.

As to the third point, if your camp has been placed behind a stockade so as to avoid open battle unless it suit your convenience and is to your advantage, I claim that in this case you are ordinarily no better off in regard to preventing an engagement than was the case in the old days, and that there are times when, on account of artillery, you may be at a greater disadvantage. For, should the enemy come upon you and have a slight advantage in position, as may easily happen should he find himself on higher ground than yours; or should you on his arriving not yet have made your trenches and dug yourself well in; straightway, and without your being able to do anything about it, he will dislodge you and you will have to quit your fortified position and join battle. This happened to the Spaniards at the battle of Ravenna. They had fortified themselves on the banks of the Ronco, but the earthworks they had thrown up were not sufficiently high and the French had a slight advantage in position, so that they were compelled by artillery to quit their fortifications and join battle. But suppose, as should usually be the case, that the site you have chosen for the camp is above that occupied by the enemy and that its earthworks are good and strong, so that, owing to your position and the other preparations you have made, the enemy does not dare to attack, it will be found that in such a case recourse will be had to the methods that were used in ancient times when someone had his army in a position in which it could not be attacked, namely, to scouring the country, taking or laying siege to towns that are friendly to you, and cutting off your supplies, so that you will be forced under such conditions to leave your camp and come out into the open, where artillery, as I shall presently point out, cannot do much. In view, therefore, of the reasons for which the Romans made war, and seeing that almost all their wars were of the offensive and not of the defensive type, it would seem that what we have said above holds good, namely, that it would have been to their advantage and would have speeded up their conquests, had there been artillery in those days.

As to the second charge, which alleges that men cannot display their valour as they used to do of old, on account of artillery, I admit it is true that, where men in small detachments have to expose themselves, there is greater danger now than then, should they have to scale the walls of a town or to make an assault of this kind not with a compact body of troops but individually, first one appearing and then another. It is also true that the officers and generals of an army are more exposed to the danger of death now than then, since anywhere they may come under artillery fire. Nor does it help them to be in the last squadron or to be supported by very brave men. One finds, none the less, that rarely does either of these two dangers occasion any out-of-the-way loss. For the walls of well-fortified towns cannot be scaled, nor are attacks on them made with weak troops. If a town is to be taken, it has to be besieged, just as it was of old. Nor, even when it is taken by assault are the dangers much greater now than they were then, for the defenders of towns even in those days did not lack equipment for launching projectiles, which, if not so terrifying, were no less effective in the matter of killing men. As to the death of officers and army commanders, in the last twenty-four years during which there have been wars in Italy, there have been fewer cases than there were during ten years of war in olden times. For, except for Count Ludovico della Mirandola, who was killed at Ferrara when the Venetians attacked that state a few years ago, and for the Duke of Nemours, who was killed abroad at Cerignuola, artillery has not killed anybody; for Monsieur de Foix was killed with a sword, not by a cannon-ball. Hence if men do not, as individuals, display their valour, it is not due to artillery, but to bad methods and to the weakness of [modern] armies, for since they lack valour as a whole, they cannot display it in the part.

To their third allegation which is that it is impossible to bring about a hand-to-hand fight and that war will eventually become a matter of artillery, I reply that this statement is altogether false, and will always be looked on as false by those who want their armies to display in their operations the virtue of ancient times. For it behoves him who wants to form a good army, to accustom his men by means of sham fights or real fights to engage the enemy at close quarters, sword in hand. Hence he should rely more on infantry than on cavalry, for reasons which will presently be given. And, if he does rely on infantry, trained as we have said, artillery becomes quite useless, since it is easier for infantry when engaging the enemy to avoid cannon-balls than it was of old for them to avoid an attack by elephants or by chariots armed with scythes, or other unfamiliar weapons such as the Roman infantry had to encounter. Against such devices they always found a remedy; and against artillery would the more easily have found a remedy in that the time during which it may harm you is shorter than that during which elephants and scythed chariots could do you harm. For the latter throw you into disorder during a battle, whereas the former is a nuisance only before the fight begins; and this nuisance infantry easily avoid either by availing themselves of such cover as the site offers or by lying flat on the ground when a volley comes. Experience, however, has shown that this is unnecessary, especially as a defence against heavy artillery; for with heavy artillery the range cannot be so nicely adjusted. Hence either the fire is too high, and does not get you, or it is too low and falls short of you.

Again, when armies come to hand-to-hand conflict, it is as clear as the day that neither heavy nor light artillery can hurt you. For if the enemy place it in front, you capture it; and, if he puts it behind, it hits his own folk before it hits you; while on the flanks it cannot do you so much damage but that you can go and get it, so that in the end it all comes to much the same thing. Nor is there much question about this. For it is clear from the case of the Swiss, who at Novara in 1513 were without either artillery or cavalry, yet went for the French army, which was supported by artillery in a fortified position, and found no difficulty on this account in breaking it up.

The reason for this, besides what I said above, is that, if artillery is to function, it must be protected either by walls or trenches or earthworks, and, if either form of protection is lacking, it either gets taken or becomes useless, just as happens when men have to defend it in pitched battles and open engagements. Nor can it be used on the flanks except in the way the ancients used projectile launching devices. Such instruments were then placed outside the main body, in order that they might function outside the ranks, and, should those who used them be overcome at any time by cavalry or other forces, they took refuge behind the regular troops. Those who expect anything more from artillery do not understand it properly and place their trust in what can easily let them down. And if by using artillery the Turk gained a victory over Sophy and the Sultan, it was solely in virtue of the panic caused among their cavalry by its unfamiliar noise.

On coming, then, to the end of this discourse, my conclusion is that artillery is useful to an army provided it be backed by valour such as was displayed of old; but, without this, it is of not the least use against a valorous army.

That Infantry should be more highly esteemed than Cavalry is shown by the Authority of the Romans and by the Example of Ancient Military Practice

It is possible to give many reasons and to cite many cases showing clearly how much greater esteem the Romans had for foot-soldiers than for cavalry in all military operations, and how upon this basis they drew up all plans for their forces. Numerous instances illustrate this; among others the battle fought with the Latins near Lake Regillus, where, when the Roman army began to give way, to support them some troops on horseback were ordered to dismount and fight on foot, by which means the battle was renewed and a victory gained. From which it is obvious that the Romans had more confidence in their men when on foot than when mounted. They used this expedient in many other battles, and always found it the best remedy in dangerous situations.

Nor can this be countered by the opinion expressed by Hannibal when during the battle of Cannae he noticed that the consuls had made their cavalry dismount, and joked about it, saying: '*Quam mallem vinctos mihi traderent equites,*' i.e. 'I should have liked it better had they handed the horsemen over to me bound.' Though this opinion is voiced by a first-class man, yet, if it be a question of authority, one should put more credence in a Roman republic and in the many first-class generals who were in it than in Hannibal alone. Furthermore, apart from an appeal to authority, sound reasons can be adduced; for a foot-soldier can get to many places to which a mounted man cannot go; infantry can be taught to keep their ranks, and, when broken, know how to re-form them, whereas it is difficult for cavalry to keep their ranks, and impossible for them to re-form when their ranks are disorganized. Besides which, one finds that horses, like men, sometimes have little spirit and sometimes a great deal, and quite often it happens that a spirited horse is ridden by a timid man and a timid horse by a man of spirit; and of whichever kind the disparity be, the result is subversive of utility and order.

Infantry, when well drawn up, can easily break cavalry, but with difficulty are routed by them. This view is corroborated not only by many instances, both ancient and modern, but also by authors who prescribe rules for the conduct of civic affairs and in them show that wars were first fought with cavalry, since there were then no rules for drawing up infantry; but when these were made, it was at once recognized that infantry are more useful than cavalry. But it does not follow from this that cavalry is not essential to an army alike for the purpose of scouting, of raiding and pillaging the country, of pursuing the enemy when in flight, and again as a partial counterpoise to the cavalry of the adversary: but it is infantry that should constitute the basis and sinews of an army and that should be held in the higher esteem.

Among the sins committed by Italian princes who have made Italy the slave of the foreigner, there is none more grave than that of having held this arm of small account and of having devoted all their attention to mounted troops. This mismanagement is due to the perversity of captains and to the ignorance of those who hold office. For the Italian militia having lost all official status during the last twenty-five years had become like soldiers of fortune. It occurred to the militia that their reputation would be made if they had the armed forces while the rulers had none. Since, then, they could not maintain a large number of infantry continually in their pay and they had no subjects of whom they could avail themselves, and since a small number would not make their reputation, they turned to cavalry; for with two or three hundred cavalry in his pay, the reputation of a *condottiere* was safe, and the pay was not such as to prevent him getting it from ministers of state. So the more easily to attain their end and to keep up their reputation they made light of all the esteem and repute in which infantry was held, and applied it instead to their own cavalry: an abuse which has grown to such an extent that even of the largest armies the infantry constitute but a fraction. It is this practice, conjoined with numerous other abuses associated with it, that has made the Italian militia so weak that Italy has become an easy prey, downtrodden by all the ultramontanes.

To show yet more clearly what a mistake it is to prefer cavalry to infantry, I shall take another example from Rome. The Romans were encamped before Sora. From the town there came forth a troop of cavalry to attack their camp. The Roman master of horse advanced to meet them with his cavalry. When they met, luck would have it that at their first encounter the officers commanding both bodies of troops were killed. Though without their leaders, the fight none the less went on, and that they might the more easily get the better of their foes, the Romans dismounted, and forced the enemy's cavalry in order to defend themselves, to do the same; by which means the Romans gained the victory. Than this example none shows better how much more virtue there is in infantry than in cavalry; for in other actions the consuls made the Roman cavalry dismount that they might help the infantry who were hard pressed and were in need of support; but in this case they dismounted, not to help the infantry, nor yet to engage the enemy's foot-soldiers, but because, while fighting as cavalry against cavalry, it occurred to them that, since as cavalry they could not prevail, they might win more easily by dismounting.

Whence I infer that it is only with the greatest difficulty that infantry when properly drawn up, can be overcome except by other infantry.

Crassus and Mark Antony, two Romans, overran the domains of the Parthians for many days with very few cavalry but plenty of infantry, though against them they had vast numbers of Parthian cavalry. Crassus with part of the army got killed, but Mark Antony fought valiantly and escaped. None the less, in the misfortunes the Romans suffered, we see how much more value infantry were than cavalry, for the country was vast, mountains scarce, streams very scarce, the sea far away, and no conveniences at hand; yet Mark Antony, as the Parthians themselves admitted, saved himself by his outstanding virtue; nor did the Parthian cavalry, numerous as it was, ever dare to try conclusions with his army. And, if Crassus was left behind, he who studies closely the record of his doings, will see that it was by deceit rather than by force that he was undone, for, in spite of all his troubles, the Parthians never ventured to attack him. On the contrary, they always went roaming about, intercepting his convoys, making promises which they did not keep, till they had reduced him to dire extremity.

I should have been at more pains, I think, to prove that the 'virtue' of infantry is more potent than that of cavalry if there had not been so many recent examples which provide abundant evidence of this. There were the nine thousand Swiss we have already mentioned, who at Novara proceeded to attack ten thousand cavalry and as many infantry, and beat them; for the cavalry could not get at them, and they thought little of the infantry, since it consisted for the most part of Gascons and was badly organized. Then there were the twenty-six thousand Swiss who went as far as Milan to look for Francis, king of France, who had with him twenty thousand cavalry, forty thousand infantry, and a hundred pieces of artillery; and if they did not win the day as they had done at Novara, they fought valiantly for two days, and, though routed, got away with half their forces. Marcus Regulus Atilius had the courage to oppose not only cavalry, but elephants, with infantry; and, if his project did not succeed, it was not because his infantry were so lacking in virtue, that he had not sufficient confidence in them to believe that they would overcome the difficulty. I repeat, then, that to get the better of well-disciplined infantry it is necessary to bring against them better disciplined infantry; otherwise the case is plainly hopeless.

In the days of Philip Visconti, Duke of Milan, there descended on Lombardy about sixteen thousand Swiss. Whereupon the Duke, whose forces were then commanded by Carmignuola, sent him with about a thousand cavalry and a few infantry to meet them. Carmignuola, unacquainted with their way of fighting, attacked them with his cavalry, assuming that he would be able to break them at once. But they stood firm, and, having lost many of his men, he retired. Being, however, a very brave man, who knew how to take fresh chances when circumstances changed, as soon as reinforcements came along to make up his strength, he went to meet them, told all his men-at-arms to dismount, and, putting them at the head of his infantry, set out to attack the Swiss. For whom there was no escape, because Carmignuola's men-at-arms having dismounted and being well protected by armour, they could easily pierce the ranks of the Swiss without suffering any harm, and, having got through, could easily overcome them. The result was that of all the Swiss there remained alive only those whom the humanity of Carmignuola chose to spare.

I believe many are aware of the difference in virtue that exists between these two kinds of troops, but so unhappy are these our times that neither ancient nor modern examples nor its being admittedly a mistake is sufficient to make modern rulers revise their point of view and realize that, if a province or a state is to keep up its military reputation, it is essential to resuscitate these services, to have them at hand, to restore their credit, to put fresh life into them, so that they may bring to the ruler both life and reputation. But, as rulers have departed from these ways, so they have departed from others mentioned above, and in consequence acquisitions do harm to a state instead of contributing to its greatness, as will presently be pointed out.

Mistakes often made in connection with war

Fortresses in General are much more Harmful than Useful

To the wiseacres of our times it may perhaps seem a foolish thing that when the Romans wanted to ensure the loyalty of the people of Latium and the city of Privernum it did not occur to them to build any sort of fortress to curb them and keep them loyal, especially as in Florence it is an accepted principle, so our wiseacres say, that Pisa and other such cities should be held by means of fortresses. Had the Romans been of their calibre, it would undoubtedly have occurred to them to build fortresses, but since their virtue, judgement, and power was of different order they did not do so. So long as Rome enjoyed freedom and was loyal to her institutions and to her efficient constitution she never held either cities or provinces by means of fortresses save where they were already built. In view, then, of the way the Romans acted in this matter and of the way rulers act today, it seems to me worth while considering whether it is good to build fortresses and whether they are harmful or useful to those who build them.

It must be borne in mind, then, that fortresses are constructed as a defence either against enemies or against subjects. In the first case they are unnecessary, and in the second case harmful. Let us begin by explaining why in the second case they are harmful. I maintain that when a prince or a republic is afraid of its subjects and fears they may rebel, the root cause of this fear must lie in the hatred which such subjects have for their rulers: a hatred which is due to their misbehaviour; and a misbehaviour which is due to their fancying they can hold them by force, or to their foolish way of governing them. And one of the things that makes rulers believe in force is the fact that they have fortresses to fall back on. For when mismanagement gives rise to hatred it is mainly due to a prince or a republic having fortresses; and, when this is the case, fortresses are far more harmful than useful. For, in the first place, they make you more foolhardy and violent in dealing with your subjects, as has been said. Next, they do not afford you internally that security you fancy they do. For no force and no violence is of the least use in controlling your people except under one of two conditions: either you have a good army which you can put in the field, as the Romans had; or your people are so exhausted, spent, disorganized and divided, that they cannot unite to do you hurt. For if you reduce them to poverty, 'though despoiled, they still have arms', and, if you disarm them, 'their fury will provide them with arms'. If you kill their leaders and suppress all other signs of insurrection, like the heads of the Hydra other leaders will arise. If you erect fortresses, they are useful in time of peace because they give you more courage in ill-treating your subjects, but in time of war they are quite useless, for they will be attacked both by your enemies and by your subjects, and against both it is impossible for them to stand. And if there ever was a time when they were useless, it is now on account of artillery, for against its fire it is impossible to defend such small places where there are no embankments behind which men can retire, as we have shown above.

In discussing this question I am going to particularize. Do you, my prince, with your fortresses want to keep a firm hand on the people in your city? Do you, be you a prince or a republic, want to tighten your grip on a city you have taken during a war? I tell you, if you be a prince, that as a means of controlling your citizens, nothing can be more futile than a fortress for the reasons I have given: it makes you quicker to use, and less careful in using, harsh measures, and by such measures you make them long for your downfall, and they become so furious that, for this very reason, your fortress will afford you no protection. So obvious is this, that a wise and good prince never constructs fortresses if he wants to remain good and to avoid providing his sons with a reason for wanting to become bad, for he would have them rely not on fortresses, but on their subjects' goodwill.

And if Count Francesco Sforza, having become Duke of Milan, was reputed a wise man, and yet built a fortress in Milan, I maintain that in this he was not wise, and the result has proved that this fortress did harm to his heirs instead of affording them security. For with a fortress they thought they were safe and could oppress their citizens and subjects, so lost no opportunity of doing them violence; with the result that they came to be detested beyond all measure, and lost their state to the first enemy who attacked them. Nor was this fortress any protection or of any service to them in time of war, while in time of peace it did them much harm, since, if they had not had it, yet had been so unwise as to treat their citizens harshly, they would have realized their danger sooner and would have withdrawn from it. In which case they would have been able to put up a more spirited resistance to the French attack with loyal subjects but without a fortress than with a fortress and disloyal subjects.

In no way, then, do fortresses help you, for you will lose them either through the treachery of their keepers, or by some violent attack, or, by their being starved out. While, if you do want them to help you, and to enable you to recover a state you have lost, in which there remains to you only a fortress, you must have an army with which to attack those who have driven you out, and when you have such an army, you will recover your state anyhow, even if there be no fortress there; and this the more easily when your men are friendly and have not been badly treated owing to the arrogance a fortress instils. Experience then shows that this Milanese fortress was not the least use either to the Sforzas or to the French when with either of them things went wrong. On the contrary, to both it brought disaster and ruin in that it prevented them from considering whether there might not be a more honest way of maintaining their position.

Guidobaldo, Duke of Urbino, the son of Frederick, who was highly esteemed in his day as an army commander, was expelled from his state by Caesar Borgia, the son of Pope Alexander VI. When later, owing to an accident, he got back, he had all the fortresses in that district razed to the ground since he thought them mischievous.

For with respect to his people who were fond of him, he did not need fortresses and, so far as his enemies were concerned, he realized he could not protect the fortresses, since he would require to have an army in the field to defend them. So he resolved to get rid of them.

Pope Julius, when he had expelled the Bentivogli from Bologna, erected a fortress in that city, and afterwards caused its inhabitants to be cruelly oppressed by one of his governors so that they rebelled; and straightaway he lost the fortress, which thus did not help him, but harmed him in as much as, had he acted otherwise, it would have helped him.

Niccolò da Castello, father of the Vitelli, on returning to his country from which he had been exiled, at once pulled down two fortresses which had been built there by Pope Sixtus IV, for he held that it was not the fortress, but the affection of his people which would preserve his state for him.

But of all such cases the most recent and the most noteworthy in every way as illustrating the futility of building fortresses and the utility of demolishing them, is what happened at Genoa not long ago. Everybody knows that in 1507 Genoa rebelled against Louis XII, King of France, who came in person with all his forces to reconquer it, and that, on recovering it, he constructed a fortress stronger than any at present known, since, situated on the point of a hill which juts into the sea, called by the Genoese Codefà, it was, owing to its position and to a number of other circumstances, impregnable, and commanded the port and a large part of the city of Genoa. It none the less came about that in 1512, when the French were driven from Italy, Genoa rebelled, despite the fortress; Ottaviano Fregoso seized the government; and, after a siege of sixteen months in which he used all possible devices, he starved the fortress out. Everyone then expected, and many advised, that it should be kept as a refuge in case of emergency, but Fregoso, like a prudent man, destroyed it, for he recognized that it is not fortresses but the wills of men that keep rulers in power. Thus, instead of relying on a fortress, he relied on virtue and sound sense, and so held his position and holds it still. And, whereas to change the government of Genoa, a thousand infantry used to suffice, its adversaries have since attacked it with ten thousand and have done it no harm. Hence one sees that dismantling a fortress did not hurt Ottaviano, and erecting one did not help the king. For so long as he could come with an army into Italy, he could recover Genoa without having a fortress there; but, when he could not come into Italy with an army, he could not hold Genoa, though he had the fortress. Thus, constructing the fortress was expensive to the king, and losing it shameful; whereas to Ottaviano the reconquering of the fortress brought glory and the demolishing of it advantage.

We come now to republics which erect fortresses not in their native land but in towns which they have acquired. If the instances already given, of France and of Genoa, do not suffice to show the fallacy involved, it should be enough if I cite those of Florence and Pisa. The Florentines erected fortresses to hold the city of Pisa, not considering that, since the Pisans had always been hostile to Florentine power, had enjoyed freedom and regarded rebellion as a means to freedom, it was necessary, if they were to retain Pisa, to adopt the Roman method, i.e. either to make it an ally or to destroy it. For the virtue of the fortresses became evident on the arrival of King Charles, to whom they surrendered owing either to the bad faith of their custodians or for fear of worse to come. Whereas if there had been no fortresses, the Florentines would not have based on them their power to hold Pisa; nor would the king have been able by means of them to deprive the Florentines of that city; for the means they had taken thus far might perchance have enabled them to keep it, and unquestionably would not have proved more disastrous than the fortresses.

I conclude, therefore, that for the purpose of holding one's own country fortresses are hurtful, and that for the purpose of holding acquired towns they are futile. The authority of the Romans is enough for me here, for round the towns they wanted to hold by force they did not build walls but pulled them down. And, if against this my view anyone should cite in ancient times the case of Tarentum, and in modern times Brescia, both of which places were regained, thanks to fortresses, after their subjects had revolted, I answer thus. To recover Tarentum Fabius Maximus, at the beginning of his year of office, was sent with a whole army, which would have sufficed for its recovery even if there had been no fortress there; and though Fabius made use of it, if it had not been there he would have adopted other means which would have produced the same effect. What use there is in a fortress I do not know, if, to recover a town, one needs a consular army and a Fabius Maximus to command it. Moreover, that the Romans would have recovered it in any case, is seen from the example of Capua, where there was no fortress, but which the Romans retook by the valour of the army.

But let us turn to Brescia. I maintain that what happened in that rebellion is a rare occurrence. Rarely when a town rebels does it happen that the fortress remains in your hands and that you have a large army in the neighbourhood, as the French then had. For Monsieur de Foix, the king's commander, had an army at Bologna, and when he heard that Brescia was lost, he went without delay to deal with the revolt, in three days reached Brescia, and with assistance from the fortress recovered the town. Here again, then, for the fortress at Brescia to be of any use, it needed a Monsieur de Foix and a French army to relieve it after three days march. The case of Brescia, therefore, is not enough to refute examples of the opposite kind; for in wars recently waged, numbers of fortresses have been taken and retaken with the same fortune that has attended the taking and retaking of open country, not only in Lombardy, but in the Romagna, in the kingdom of Naples, and in every part of Italy.

As to building fortresses for defence against external foes, I maintain that they are unnecessary where peoples or kingdoms have good armies and that to those who have no such armies they are useless; for good armies without fortresses suffice for defence, and fortresses without good armies are no defence. This is borne out by the experience of men of high repute as rulers and in other matters, for instance, the Romans and the Spartans; for if the Romans did not build fortresses, the Spartans not only abstained from doing this, but did not permit their cities to have walls, because they chose to rely for defence on the virtue of the individual, and wanted no other. Hence, when a Spartan was asked by an Athenian whether the walls of Athens did not look fine, he answered: 'Quite! provided it be ladies who live there.'

The ruler, then, who has good armies, may sometimes find it useful, though not essential, to have fortresses on the coast and on the frontiers of his domains to hold off the attack of an enemy till he gets properly going. But, if he has not a good army, to have fortresses within his state or on its frontiers is either harmful or useless: harmful because he so easily loses them and, when lost, they make war on him; or, if they should chance to be so strong that the enemy cannot capture them, they get left behind by the hostile army and so come to be useless. For, when good armies do not meet with very strong opposition, on entering a country they pay no attention to cities and fortresses, which they may leave behind them. We see this in ancient history just as we have seen it done by Francesco Maria, who in quite recent times, when on his way to attack Urbino, left behind him ten of the enemy's cities, without bothering about them.

The ruler, then, who can muster a good army, can do without fortresses, and the ruler who has not a good army had better not build them. The best thing he can do is to fortify the city where he dwells, to keep it provisioned and its inhabitants well disposed, so as to hold off an enemy's attack till he can either come to terms or get outside help to relieve him. All other plans are expensive in time of peace and useless in time of war. In view, then, of all I have said, it will be seen that, as the Romans were wise in their other institutions, so, too, were they prudent when they decided in the case of the Latins and the Privernates to dispense with fortresses and took more virtuous and wiser means of securing their loyalty.

To attack a Divided City in the Hope that its Divisions will facilitate the Conquest of it is Bad Policy

There was so much discord between the plebs and the nobility in the Roman republic that the Veientes, in conjunction with the Etruscans, thought this disunion would enable them to destroy the power of Rome. Having, therefore, formed an army and invaded Roman territory, the senate sent Gaius Manlius and Marcus Fabius to engage them. When the army they were leading drew near to the army of the Veientes, the latter kept on attacking and vilifying the Roman name with insults and abuse. And so great was their rashness and insolence that the Romans became united instead of disunited, and, when it came to a fight, broke and defeated the enemy. Thus one sees, as we have said above, how mistaken men are when in coming to decisions they rely on discord, and how often, when they think they have a sure thing they lose. The Veientes thought that if they attacked the Romans, when disunited, they would overcome them; but their attack caused the Romans to unite and brought about their own ruin. For discord in a republic is usually due to idleness and peace, and unity to fear and to war. Had the Veientes been wise, then, the more disunited they found the Romans to be, the more studiously should they have refrained from going to war with them, and have striven to get the better of them by the artifices men use in time of peace.

The way to set about this is to win the confidence of the city which is disunited; and, so long as they do not come to blows, to act as arbitrator between the parties, and, when they do come to blows, to give tardy support to the weaker party, both with a view to keeping them at it and wearing them out; and, again, because stronger measures would leave no room for any to doubt that you were out to subjugate them and make yourself their ruler. When this scheme is well carried out, it will happen, as always, that the end you have in view will be attained. The city of Pistoia, as I have said in another discourse and apropos of another topic, was acquired by the republic of Florence by just such an artifice; for it was divided and the Florentines supported now one, now the other party and, without making themselves obnoxious to either, led them on until they got sick of their turbulent way of living and in the end came to throw themselves voluntarily into the arms of Florence.

The city of Siena has never changed its form of government with the help of the Florentines except when their help was weak and infrequent; for, when it was frequent and strong, its effect was to make that city united in defence of the government in power.

I wish to add to the above-mentioned examples a further example. Filippo Visconti, Duke of Milan, several times made war on the Florentines, relying on their disunion, and in all cases came out the loser, so that when he was bewailing these attacks, he used to say that the follies of the Florentines had involved him in an expenditure of two millions in gold to no purpose.

It remained, then, that the Veientes and the Tuscans were mistaken on this point, as was said above, so that in the end there came a battle when the Romans conquered them. And in like manner will others find themselves mistaken, should they imagine that by such means and in such circumstances they can bring a people into subjection.

Scorn and abuse arouse Hatred against those who indulge in them without bringing them any Advantage

I hold it to be a sign of great prudence in men to refrain alike from threats and from the use of insulting language, for neither of these things deprives the enemy of his power, but the first puts him more on his guard, while the other intensifies his hatred of you and makes him more industrious in devising means to harm you. This is seen in the case of the Veientes, whom we were discussing in the previous chapter. Besides the injury done by the war, they abused the Romans by word of mouth, a thing which every sensible general should prevent his soldiers from doing, for such language does but exasperate the enemy and move him to vengeance, nor, as has been said, does it in any way interfere with his attack: so that in fact they are weapons which turn against you.

Of this a notable instance occurred in Asia. When Cobades, the Persian commander, had been besieging

Amida for a considerable time, he grew weary of the tiresome business and decided to withdraw. While he was striking camp the townsmen, exhilarated by their victory, all climbed on the walls and used every sort of abuse, calumniating and accusing and upbraiding the enemy for his cowardice and poltroonery. This so annoyed Cobades that he changed his mind, and, indignant at the injustice, returned to the siege and in a few days had taken and sacked the city.

The same thing happened to the Veientes, who, as I have said, were not content to make war on the Romans, but also spoke of them contemptuously, going up to the stockade surrounding their camp and shouting abuse at them. This annoyed the troops much more than the fighting did; so that, whereas they had at first fought unwillingly, they now pressed the consuls to join battle, with the result that the Veientes, like those mentioned above, were punished for their contumacy as they deserved. Good army commanders and good republican rulers should take all appropriate measures to prevent the use of abusive language and taunts, whether in the city or in their army, and whether used one towards another or towards the enemy. For, if used towards the enemy, there ensue the aforesaid inconveniences, and still worse inconveniences if used one towards the other, unless precautions be taken, as they always have been by prudent men.

When the Roman legions, left in Capua, conspired against the Capuans, as will be narrated in due course, and in connection with this conspiracy a mutiny arose, subsequently quelled by Valerius Corvinus, among other points in the convention he drew up, it prescribed the severest penalties on those who should reproach any of the troops for having taken part in the mutiny.

Tiberius Gracchus, who, during the war with Hannibal, had been put in command of a certain number of slaves, whom, owing to the shortage of men, the Romans had armed, made a special point of the capital punishment he prescribed for anyone who should reproach any slave with his servitude.

We see, then, how harmful the Romans thought it to calumniate others or to reproach them for a shameful deed, as has been said, for than this there is nothing that inflames the mind more, or arouses greater indignation, whether the taunt be true or be said in jest, 'For smart sayings, when they border on the truth, leave a bitter taste behind them.'

Prudent Princes and Republics should be content with Victory, for, when they are not content with it, they usually lose

Speaking to the disparagement of an enemy is usually due to the arrogance aroused in you by victory or by the false hope of victory. False hopes of this kind not only cause men to make mistakes in what they say, but also in what they do. For, when such hopes enter men's breasts, they cause them to dispense with caution, and often to miss the chance of obtaining a sure thing in the hope, but by no means the certainty, of improving on it. This matter is worth considering, since very often men make mistakes in regard to it, detrimental to their Tyre, elated with success, not only refused to accept his terms, but killed the envoy who came to arrange matters. Whereupon Alexander, becoming indignant, put such life into the siege that he took and demolished the city, and either killed or made slaves of its inhabitants.

In 1512 a Spanish army invaded the dominions of Florence with a view to restoring the Medici and levying a tax on the city, acting on behalf of fifth columnists who had led them to expect that, once they had crossed the border, they would take up arms in their favour. On entering the plain [of the Arno] they found none of them, and, as they were short of provisions, they made overtures of peace. The people of Florence were too proud to accept them. Hence the loss of Prato, and the ruin of that state.

Rulers of states, when attacked, therefore, cannot make a greater mistake than to refuse to come to terms when the forces attacking them are a good deal stronger than their own, especially if the overtures are made by the enemy: for the terms will never be so hard but that in them some benefit will accrue to those who accept them, so that in a way they will share in the victory. The people of Tyre, for instance, should have been content that Alexander had accepted the conditions which he had at first refused, and the victory thus gained would have been considerable, since with their armed forces they had compelled a great man to condescend to their wishes. It should, in like manner, have sufficed the people of Florence that the Spanish army had yielded to any of their demands instead of fulfilling all their own, for this, too, would have been a considerable victory. For what the Spanish army wanted was to change the form of government in Florence, to put an end to its attachment to France, and to levy tribute. If of these three things the Spaniards had gained the last two, and the people of Florence had gained the first, that is the retention of their form of government, each would have acquired a certain honour and a certain satisfaction; nor would the people have been likely to trouble much about the other two things, so long as their lives were safe. Nay, even had they seen there was a good, and almost certain, chance of a greater victory, they should not have placed themselves wholly at the discretion of fortune and ventured their last stake, which it is never wise to risk unless driven to it.

When Hannibal, who had enjoyed great glory in Italy for sixteen years, left it on being recalled by the Carthaginians to help his own country, he found Hasdrubal and Syphax routed, the kingdom of Numidia lost, and the Carthaginians cooped up within their own walls, destitute of hope except what he and his army should bring. Realizing that his country was reduced to its last stake, he was determined not to risk that till he had tried all other remedies, and so was not ashamed to sue for peace, since he was convinced that, if there was any hope at all for his country, it lay in this and not in war. When peace was refused, he did not decline to fight though bound to lose, since he felt that he could still win, but if he had to lose, he could at least lose gloriously. If, then, Hannibal, who was so full of virtuosity, and had his army still intact, preferred peace to war when he saw that, by losing, his country would be enslaved, what should a man do who has neither the efficiency nor the experience of Hannibal? Yet there are men who make this mistake, in that to their hopes they set no bound, and are ruined because they rely on such hopes and take no account of other things.

Rome's dealings with neighbouring states and cities in peace and war

How Dangerous it is for a Republic or a Prince not to avenge an Injury done either to the Public or to a Private Person

What is likely to make men indignant with others may easily be learnt from what happened to the Romans when they sent the three Fabii as ambassadors to the Gauls, who were about to attack Tuscany and, in particular, Clusium. The people of Clusium had appealed to Rome for help against the Gauls. Hence the Romans sent the three Fabii as ambassadors to the Gauls to insist in the name of the Roman republic on their abstaining from a war with the Tuscans. When they arrived at their destination the ambassadors, who were better at acting than speaking, found the Gauls and the Tuscans about to join battle, whereupon they were the foremost to enter the fray. It thus came about that when the Gauls became aware of this, their annoyance with the Tuscans was turned against the Romans. And their indignation was intensified when the Gauls, having complained to the Roman senate through their ambassadors of this unfairness and demanded that the aforesaid Fabii be handed over to them to compensate for the harm they had done, they were not only not handed over or punished in some other way, but an election was held in which they were made tribunes with consular power. Consequently when the Gauls saw those being honoured who ought to have been punished, they took it as an affront and an indignity offered to themselves, and, inflamed with indignation and anger, marched on Rome and took it, except for the Capitol. A disaster which the Romans brought on themselves through their disregard of justice, for since their ambassadors had offended 'against the Law of Nations', they should have been punished, instead of being honoured.

This leads one to consider how important it is for every republic and every prince to take account of such offences, not only when an injury is done to a whole people, but also when it affects an individual. For if an individual is grievously offended either by the public or by a private person, and does not receive due satisfaction, he will, if he lives in a republic, seek to avenge himself, even if it lead to the ruin of that republic; and, if he lives under a prince and has a spark of manliness, will never rest content till he has in some way or other wreaked vengeance on him even though he sees that, in doing so, he will bring disaster on himself.

In verification of this there is no finer or more relevant instance than that of Philip, king of Macedon, the father of Alexander, in whose court there was a handsome and noble young man, Pausanias. With him Attalus, one of the chief men in Philip's entourage, was enamoured, and had on several occasions sought to get him to assent, but found that he had no liking for such things; so, seeing that he could not get what he wanted otherwise, he decided to set a trap for him and to use force. He gave, therefore, a great banquet, which Pausanias and other noble barons attended, and, when they had had their fill of food and wine, he had him seized and bound; then he not only used force in order to gratify his lust, but, to his greater shame, got others to treat him in the same disgusting way. Of this affront Pausanias complained several times to Philip, who, having kept him for a time in expectation of vengeance, not only did not avenge him, but made Attalus governor of a Grecian province. Pausanias, therefore, seeing his enemy honoured instead of being punished, gave full vent to his indignation not only against the perpetrator of the deed, but against Philip who had not avenged it. So, one morning, the day of the solemn wedding of Philip's daughter, who was being married to Alexander of Epirus, he killed Philip as he was going to the temple for the celebration standing between the two Alexanders, his son and his son-in-law. Of this incident, which is akin to that which happened to the Romans, all who rule should take note, so that they may never esteem any man so lightly as to think that, if injury be added to injury, the injured person will not consider how to vindicate himself, even though it involve him in all manner of dangers and entail his own downfall.

Fortune blinds Men's Minds when she does not wish them to obstruct her Designs

If one ponders well the course of human affairs, it will be seen that many events happen and many misfortunes come about, against which the heavens have not been willing that any provision at all should be made. Since this statement holds good in the case of Rome, which was conspicuous alike for virtue, religion and orderly conduct, it is no wonder that the same thing happens yet more often in cities and provinces which are lacking in these respects. There is a well-known passage in which Titus Livy shows at length and with great force the power that heaven exercises over human affairs. He says that, with a view to making the Romans recognize its power, heaven first caused the Fabii to act wrongly when sent as ambassadors to the Gauls, and by means of what they did excited the Gauls to make war on Rome; then ordained that in Rome nothing worthy of the Roman people should be done to meet their attack; for first it brought about that Camillus, who was the only hope they had in those evil days, should be sent as an exile to Ardea; then that, when the Gauls were marching on Rome, they did not appoint a dictator, as they had done many times to meet the attack of the Volsci and other enemies in the neighbourhood. It also caused them to be weak and to take no particular care in calling up troops, who were so slow in taking up arms that they scarce had time to confront the Gauls on the banks of the Allia, which was but ten miles from Rome. There the tribunes set up their camp without their accustomed diligence, since they did not inspect the site beforehand, nor surround it with trenches and stockades, nor take any other precautions, either human or divine; while in preparing for battle they made their ranks thin and weak, and neither troops nor officers behaved as Roman discipline required. No blood was shed during the battle because at the first onslaught the Romans ran away, the greater number going to Veii, and the rest retiring on Rome, where they sought refuge in the Capitol without first going home; whereupon the senate took so little thought for Rome's defence that, for one thing, they omitted to close the gates; and some of its members fled, while others went with the rest into the Capitol. Granted, in their defence of the Capitol they used some sort of discipline, for they did not pack all the useless people inside, and they got in all the corn they could, so as to be able to stand the siege; while of the use-less crowd of old men, women and children, most fled to the country round about, and the rest stayed in Rome at the mercy of the Gauls. So that no one who had read of what was done so often in years gone by and were to read what was now being done, would think they were one and the same people.

Having described all the disorders mentioned above, Titus Livy concludes with the remark: 'To such an extent does fortune blind the minds of men when she does not want them to oppose the force she is using.'

Nor can anything be more true than the conclusion Livy draws. Hence men who in this life normally either suffer great adversity or enjoy great prosperity, deserve neither praise nor blame; for one usually finds that they have been driven either to ruin or to greatness by the prospect of some great advantage which the heavens have held out, whereby they have been given the chance, or have been deprived of the chance, of being able to act virtuously. Fortune arranges this quite nicely. For, when it wants a man to take the lead in doing great things, it chooses a man of high spirits and great virtue who will seize the occasion it offers him. And in like manner, when it wants a man to bring about a great disaster, it gives precedence to men who will help to promote it; and, if anyone gets in the way, it either kills him off or deprives him of all power of doing good.

It plainly appears from Livy's evidence that, in order to make Rome greater and to lead it on to its future greatness, fortune decided it was necessary first to chastise it in a way that will be described at length in the beginning of the next book, but did not want to ruin it altogether. Hence we see that it made an exile of Camillus, but did not cause him to die; that it caused Rome to be taken, but not the Capitol; that it arranged matters so that nothing useful was thought of to help Rome, nor anything overlooked that could help in the defence of the Capitol. It brought it about that, since Rome was to be taken, the greater part of the troops which were routed at Allia, should go on to Veii, thus leaving the city without any men to defend it. But in arranging things thus, it also prepared the way for Rome's recovery; for since there was a Roman army at Veii, and Camillus was at Ardea, it became possible to make a more vigorous attempt to deliver the fatherland under a general whose career was free from the stain of defeat and whose reputation was untarnished.

In confirmation of this one might adduce further examples from modern times, but I do not think this necessary, so pass them over, since that I have given should be enough to satisfy anybody. I assert once again as a truth to which history as a whole bears witness that men may second their fortune, but cannot oppose it; that they may weave its warp, but cannot break it. Yet they should never give up, because there is always hope, though they know not the end and move towards it along roads which cross one another and as yet are unexplored; and since there is hope, they should not despair, no matter what fortune brings or in what travail they find themselves.

Really Powerful Republics and Princes do not purchase Alliances with Money, but obtain them by means of the Virtue and the Reputation of their Forces

The Romans were being besieged in the Capitol, and, though they expected help from Veii and from Camillus, were in such bad case owing to famine that they came to terms with the Gauls and agreed to pay them so much gold. They were weighing out the gold agreed upon when Camillus arrived with his army; whereupon fortune, says the historian, decided that 'the Romans should not by purchase save their lives'.

This kind of thing is not only noticeable in this case but characterizes the behaviour of this republic throughout. We never find the Romans purchasing towns, or paying in order to obtain peace. They always acquired both by virtue of their arms. Nor do I think that this has ever happened in the case of any other republic. Among other indications of the power of a strong state one looks to the terms on which it lives with its neighbours. When it is so governed that, to obtain its friendship, its neighbours become its tributaries, it is a sure sign that the state is powerful; but when the said neighbours, though inferior in strength, extract payment from it, it is a sure sign of its weakness.

As one runs through Roman history, one sees how the Massilians, the Aedui, the Rhodians, Hiero of Syracuse, king Eumenes and king Masinissa, who were neighbours with estates bordering on the empire of Rome, were ready to incur expense and pay tribute in order to obtain the friendship of Rome, and in return ask only for her protection. In weak states one finds just the opposite. To begin with, in our own state, Florence, in times past when its reputation stood at its highest, there was no lord in the Romagna who did not receive payment from it. It also made grants to the Perugians, the Castellani and all its other neighbours. Had this city been armed and strong, everything would have been just the contrary, for to secure its protection many states would have paid money to it, and would have sought to purchase its friendship, not to sell their own.

Nor are the Florentines the only people who have thus demeaned themselves since the Venetians and the King of France do the same thing; for the latter, great as his kingdom is, habitually pays tribute to the Swiss and to the King of England. This all comes from depriving the people of arms, and from the fact that this king and the other states mentioned have chosen rather to enjoy the present advantage of being able to despoil their people and of being able to avoid an imaginary rather than a real danger, instead of so acting as to secure their people's goodwill and to make their state happy for ever. A malpractice such as this, though it may bring a little temporary quiet, in time becomes the cause of crises, disaster and irremediable ruin. It would take too long to relate how often the Florentines, the Venetians, and this kingdom, have bought off wars and submitted to an ignominy which the Romans submitted to but once. It would take too long to recount how many towns the Florentines and the Venetians have purchased in which one afterwards saw disorder, and how they failed to protect with steel what gold had purchased. The Romans kept up their standards so long as they remained free; but when they fell under the yoke of the emperors, and the emperors began to behave badly and to prefer the shadow to the sun, they, too, began to make grants sometimes to the Parthians, sometimes to Germany, sometimes to other neighbouring peoples; which was the first step towards that great empire's downfall.

Such are the inconveniences, then, that arise from depriving your people of arms. And there is a worse trouble, too, for the greater the force of the enemy's attack, the weaker do you find yourself; for he who lives in the aforesaid way treats ill the subjects who reside within his domain, but treats well those who live on its confines in order to have people well disposed to keep the enemy off. It thus comes about that, in order the better to keep the enemy off, he subsidizes the lords and peoples who are his next-door neighbours, with the result that the states which he has thus kept going, offer a modicum of resistance on the frontiers, but, when the enemy has crossed them, no further remedy is available. Such states do not see that their way of proceeding is incompatible with any kind of good order. For it is the heart and the vital parts of the body that have to be strengthened, not its extremities, since without them the body can survive, but, if the former be injured, it dies; yet such states keep unarmed the heart, but arm the hands and the feet.

What this lack of order has done for Florence is clear, and may be seen any day; for when an army crosses its frontiers and gets near its heart, it finds itself without further remedy. Of it the Venetians also gave proof a few years ago, and, if their city had not been girt about by water, it would have been the end of it. In France this experience is not found so frequently, for it is so large a kingdom that it has but few enemies superior to it. None the less, when the English attacked this kingdom in 1513, the whole realm was in trepidation, and the king and everybody else thought that a single defeat would spell ruin to the king and to the state. Very different was it in the case of the Romans, for the nearer the enemy approached to Rome the greater he found the city's power of resistance to be. When Hannibal invaded Italy, one sees how, after three defeats and the death of so many generals and soldiers, it was still able, not merely to withstand the enemy, but to win the war. All this comes from having fortified well the heart, but of the extremities made less account. For of basic importance in this state were the people of Rome, the people known as Latins, the other parts of Italy associated with it, and its colonies. Thence came the vast number of soldiers which enabled it to fight and to hold the whole world. That this is so may be seen from the question asked by Hanno, the Carthaginian, of the messengers who came from Hannibal after the rout at Cannae. Having made much of Hannibal's exploits, they were asked by Hanno whether the Roman people had sent to ask for peace, and whether among the

Latins and in its colonies any town had revolted against the Romans. To both questions the answer was in the negative, whereupon Hanno remarked: 'This war, then, is still in as full swing as it was at the start.'

We see from this discourse and from what I have said in other places, how great is the difference between the procedure of present-day republics and that of ancient republics. We see, too, how, because of this, astonishing acquisitions are made and astonishing losses occur daily. For where men have but little virtue, fortune makes a great display of its power; and, since fortune changes, republics and governments frequently change; and will go on changing till someone comes along, so imbued with the love of antiquity that he regulates things in such fashion that fortune does not every time the sun turns round get a chance of showing what it can do.

How Dangerous it is to put Confidence in Refugees

It may not be amiss among other topics to show how dangerous it is to trust those who have been driven from their country, since this is a matter with which everyone who holds office has to deal. In support it is possible to adduce a noteworthy case which Titus Livy cites in his histories, though it lies outside his main topic. When Alexander the Great crossed with his army into Asia, Alexander of Epirus, a relative – in fact his uncle – went with some troops to Italy, having been invited by some Lucanian refugees who had led him to expect that through their mediation he would gain the whole of that country.

Relying on their word and on the hopes they aroused, he came to Italy and was put to death by them; for their fellow-citizens had promised that, if they would kill him, they might return to their own country. One should reflect, therefore, on the unreliability of agreements and promises made by men who find themselves shut out from their country, because in determining what such men's word is worth it must be borne in mind that, once they get a chance of returning to their country without your help, they will desert you and turn to others in spite of any promises they may have made you. While in regard to the vain promises and hopes, so intense is their desire to get back home that they naturally believe much that is false and artfully add much more: so that between what they believe and what they say they believe they fill you with a hope which is such that, if you rely on it, either you incur expense in vain or take up what will ruin you.

I propose to let this example of Alexander suffice, conjoined with that of Themistocles the Athenian, who, having been proclaimed a rebel, sought refuge with Darius in Asia; to whom he promised so much if he would but attack Greece that Darius resolved to do so. When later he was unable to fulfil these promises whether out of shame or for fear of punishment, Themistocles poisoned himself. Wherefore, if so eminent a man as Themistocles made this mistake, how much more likely are those to err who are less virtuous and let themselves be swayed by their desires and their passions. A ruler, therefore, should be slow to take up an enterprise because of what some exile has told him, for more often than not all he will get out of it is shame or most grievous harm.

And because the taking of towns by stealth and owing to information supplied by their inhabitants rarely succeeds, it does not seem to me irrelevant to discuss this in the next chapter, as also in how many ways the Romans acquired them.

On the Various Methods used by the Romans in taking Towns

Since the Romans were all keen on war, they always and on all occasions took advantage of anything, alike in the matter of expense and of any other matter, that promised to help. It was for this reason that they took care not to besiege the towns they took, for they thought this method so costly and so clumsy that its disadvantages would much more than counterbalance the advantages likely to accrue from the conquest. Hence they deemed it better and more useful to subjugate towns by any other means rather than lay siege to them, so that in all their wars and in all the years they took, there are very few instances of their having used sieges.

In order to get hold of a city, therefore, the Romans either took it by assault or got it to surrender. Their assaults were either carried out openly in strength and with violence, or by force conjoined with fraud. When storming a town openly they used two methods. Either they attacked it on all sides without first demolishing the walls, which is called 'putting a crown round the city' since the whole army surrounds it and engages it at all points; and in this way they often succeeded in taking a city, even a very large one, at the first assault, as Scipio took New Carthage in Spain. Or, when an attack failed, they set about breaking down the walls with rams and other siege implements, or made a sap by which they obtained entrance to the city, as was done when Veii was taken; or to get on a level with those defending the walls, they constructed wooden towers, or raised earthworks against the walls from without, so as to be at the same height as the defenders.

Against such assaults the city's defenders in the first case, where the attack came from all sides, were more quickly exposed to danger and had more dubious remedies. For, since many defenders were needed everywhere, either those they had were not enough to provide them all with reserves and reliefs; or, if they could, not all were equally courageous in resisting, and, if a section shirked the battle, all was lost. Hence it often happened, as I have said, that this method proved successful. But when the first assault was not successful, they did not keep it going long, because this was too dangerous for the army; for, since it covered so much ground, it could as a whole resist but feebly a sortie made by those within. The troops, too, got out of hand and grew weary; but for just once, when it was unexpected, they would try this method. When a breach was made in the walls, it was countered by means of ramparts as at the present time. And to counteract a sap, they made a countersap through which they got at the enemy either with their weapons or by other devices; of which one consisted of barrels filled with feathers to which they applied a light, and, when burning, put them in the sap so that the smoke and the stench might prevent the enemy getting through. While, if attacked from towers, they tried to destroy them by fire; and, if from earthworks, they made a hole in the lower part of the wall on which the earthwork was leaning, and drew in the earth which those outside had put there, so that, since the earth was being piled up outside and being taken away from the inside, the earthwork did not grow.

Such methods of storming a town could not be kept up for long, so they had either to raise their camp or to devise other methods of winning the war, as Scipio did when he got to Africa; for when he attacked Utica, but did not succeed in taking it, he raised his camp and sought to engage the Carthaginian armies and break them. Or they would have recourse to a siege, as they did at Veii, Capua, Carthage, Jerusalem and other towns which they took by means of sieges.

The acquiring of towns by furtive violence is illustrated in the case of Palaeopolis, which the Romans took by arrangement with fifth columnists inside. This form of attack has often been tried by the Romans and by other peoples, but has seldom succeeded. The reason is that at the smallest setback the plan breaks down, and such setbacks easily happen. For in the first place the conspiracy may be discovered before it comes to a head, and in discovering it there is not much difficulty, owing sometimes to the treachery of those who have been told of it, sometimes to practical difficulties. For you must get in touch with the enemy, with whom it is not permitted to speak unless you can find some excuse. And, should the plot not be discovered while arrangements are being made, a host of difficulties occur when the time comes for action. For if you arrive before the time appointed, or get there late, anything may upset the plot. So, too, if there occurs some unexpected noise, such as the geese made at the Capitol, or if the normal course of events is interrupted. Given the least blunder or the smallest mistake, the attack is bound to fail. In addition to which there is the darkness of the night to add to the fear of those engaged in such dangerous tasks; and the fact that most of the men who are taken on such expeditions, having had no experience of the country or of the place to which they are being led, may get muddled and faint-hearted, or upset by some tiny and accidental mishap; and any false impression is enough to make them turn tail.

Anyone more lucky in such stealthy nocturnal ventures than Aratus the Sicyonian is not to be found, yet, bold as he was in these, he was equally nervous about ventures in daylight and in the open. This we may put down to some occult virtue with which he was endowed, rather than to anything in the nature of nocturnal expeditions which makes them more fortunate than others. Though such means are frequently planned, therefore, but few arrive at fruition, and very few succeed.

When towns are acquired by surrender, the surrender may either be voluntary or compulsory. When voluntary, it is due either to some external circumstance which compels a town to seek protection under another's wing, as Capua sought Rome's; or to the desire to be well ruled, a desire evoked by the good government exercised by the prince in question over those who of their own accord have placed themselves in his hands, as was the case with the Rhodians, the Massilians and other such cities which surrendered to the Roman people. When the surrender is compulsory, it is either brought about by a long siege, as we have said above; or it is due to the continued vexation produced by raids, depredations and other annoyances, to escape which a city surrenders.

Of all the methods mentioned above, the Romans used the last more than any. For more than four hundred and fifty years they sought to tire out their neighbours by defeats in the field and by raids, and by means of treaties managed to acquire greater repute than their rivals did, as we have pointed out elsewhere. It was on this method that they always relied most, though they tried them all, but found the others fraught with danger or of no use. For sieges are long and costly, assaults of doubtful issue and risky; and conspiracies are unreliable. They also realized that, if the enemy's army was routed, they acquired a kingdom in a day; whereas, if they besieged an obstinate city, it might take years to get it.

The Romans gave to Army Commanders Discretionary Powers

If one is to profit from the perusal of Livy's history one ought, I think, to take account of all the modes of procedure used by the people and senate of Rome and among other points worthy of notice there is the authority we find them giving to their consuls, dictators and other army commanders when in the field. It was of a very high order, for the senate reserved to itself only the power to initiate fresh wars and to confirm peace treaties. All else was left to the discretion and power of the consul. For, when the people and senate had decided to go to war, against the Latins, for instance, they left everything else to the discretion of the consul, who could either give battle or not give it, and attack this or that town as he thought fit.

This is confirmed by numerous examples, but especially by what occurred in an expedition against the Tuscans. The consul, Fabius, had defeated those who were near Sutrium, and was planning next to lead his army through the Ciminian forest *en route* for Tuscany. About this, not only did he not consult the senate, but he did not even inform them, though the war was to be carried on in a new, unexplored and dangerous country. Further confirmation is afforded by the action the senate here took, which was of the opposite kind; for, when they heard of the victory which Fabius had gained and wondered whether his next step would be to pass through the said forest into Tuscany, they thought it best not to run the risk this war would entail, and so sent two legates to Fabius to stop him from going on to Tuscany. But, when they arrived, he had already got there and had won a victory, so that, instead of preventing a war, the legates came home bringing news of a conquest and of glory won.

Whoever considers carefully this technique will see that it was very wise to make use of it. For, if the senate had required a consul in conducting a war to proceed step by step according as they directed, it would have made him less circumspect and slower to act, for it would have seemed to him that the glory of victory would not be wholly his, but that the senate would share in it, since it would have been carried out under its directions. Furthermore, the senate would have had to advise on matters of which it had no immediate cognizance; for, though the senators were all men of considerable experience in military matters, yet, as they were not on the spot, they would not be acquainted with the multitudinous details which it is essential to know before one can give sound advice, and so would have made numerous mistakes. This being so, they preferred that the consul should decide what to do, and that the glory should be wholly his, for they thought his actions would be so restrained and regulated by his love of glory that he would do his utmost.

To this I have the more willingly called attention, because I notice that the republics of today, such as the Venetian and the Florentine republics, act differently, for if their generals, administrators or commissioners, have to set up a piece of artillery, they want to know of it and to advise about it – a procedure as praiseworthy as are others of that ilk, which together have brought us to our present pass.

Sundry remarks on strategy, tactics, new devices and discipline

That a General cannot avoid an Engagement if the Enemy is determined to force him to it at All Costs

'Gaius Sulpicius, the dictator, when waging war with the Gauls, was unwilling to try his fortune in an engagement with an enemy whose position time and an awkward situation was steadily making worse.' When there occurs an error which all men, or most men, are liable to make, it is not a bad thing, I think, to warn them often against it. Since, therefore, as I have frequently pointed out, the way in which important matters are dealt with today does not come up to the standard of the ancients, it does not seem to me superfluous at this juncture to point it out once again. For, if there be any way in which there has been a departure from ancient customs, it is especially so in military matters, in which none of the things the ancients esteemed so highly are now done. This inconvenience is due to republics and princes having entrusted such matters to other people. To avoid danger they themselves keep clear of military operations and, though one does sometimes find a king in these days sallying forth in person, I do not on this account think that it leads him to do much else that is worthy of commendation. For when they actually do engage in military operations, they do it

88

for the sake of display and not for any praiseworthy reason. True, in that they occasionally review their troops and reserve to themselves the title of commander, they make mistakes of less moment than do republics, especially Italian republics, which rely on others and understand nothing which has to do with war, and yet in their desire to look like a prince in the eyes of the army, make decisions, and, in doing so, commit innumerable blunders.

And although some of these blunders I have discussed elsewhere, I cannot here be silent about one which is very important. When these idle princes or effeminate republics are sending one of their generals on an expedition, it seems to them that the wisest thing they can commission him to do, is on no account to engage in open battle, but, on the contrary, above all else to be on his guard against an engagement; for they think that in so doing they are emulating the prudence of Fabius Maximus who, by putting off an engagement, saved the Roman state from destruction; wherein they overlook the fact that, more often than not, such a commission is nonsensical or dangerous. The point one has to bear in mind here is that a general who proposes to remain in the field cannot avoid battle if the enemy is determined to force one on him at all costs. Hence what such a commission amounts to is just this: 'Join battle at the enemy's behest, not at your own'. For, if one wants to remain in the field and not join battle, the only safe thing to do is to put at least fifty miles between oneself and the enemy, and then to have good scouts so that, should he come your way, you may have time to get farther off. Another alternative in this case is to shut yourself up in a city. But both courses are extremely harmful. For the first leaves your country at the mercy of the enemy, and a valiant prince would sooner try his fortune in battle than prolong a war at such cost to his subjects. While the second alternative is manifestly that of a lost cause, for what it comes to is that, when you have got your army into a city, you may be besieged, and before long to be reduced by the pangs of hunger to surrender. Hence to avoid battle in either of these two ways is extremely hurtful. The plan adopted by Fabius Maximus of occupying strong positions is good so long as you have so valiant an army that the enemy does not dare come and seek you out in your position of vantage. Nor can it be said that Fabius avoided battle, but rather that he preferred to fight when he had the advantage. For, if Hannibal had gone to seek him out, he would have awaited him and made a day of it. But Hannibal did not dare to fight with him on these terms. So that it was as much Hannibal who avoided battle as Fabius; but, if either had determined at all costs to fight, the other would have had to adopt one of three courses, i.e. either to adopt one of the two courses mentioned above, or else to run away.

That what I am saying is true can be clearly seen from a host of cases, and especially in the war the Romans had with Philip of Macedon, the father of Perseus. For, when Philip was attacked by the Romans, he decided not to join battle, and, to avoid it, did at first what Fabius Maximus did in Italy: posted himself with his army on top of a mountain where he erected fortifications, thinking that the Romans would not dare to go and seek him out. But they did go, and, having fought with him, drove him from the mountain, and he, being powerless to resist, fled with the greater part of his forces. What saved him from being utterly undone was the impossible country, which prevented the Romans from following him up. Philip, therefore, still desirous of avoiding battle and being encamped in the neighbourhood of the Romans, had to get away; and, having learned by experience that, to avoid battle, it is not enough to take up a position on top of a mountain, and being averse to shutting himself up in towns, decided to take the remaining course and to put many miles between himself and the Roman camp. Hence, when the Romans were in one province, he moved to another, and, in like manner, whenever the Romans moved out, he moved in. But when at length he came to see that by prolonging the war in this way his situation was getting worse, and that, now by him, now by the enemy, his subjects were being harassed, he decided to try his fortune in battle. He thus came to an engagement with the Romans, as was proper.

It is useful then not to fight under the conditions in which Fabius' army found itself, or again in those in which Gaius Sulpicius found himself, i.e. when you have so good an army that the enemy does not dare to come and oust you from your fortified position; or when the enemy is in your country, but without having the footing there that would guarantee provisions. In this case the course adopted is useful for the reasons Livy gives when he says: 'he was unwilling to try his fortune in an engagement with the enemy so long as time and his adverse situation were daily making the enemy's position worse'. But under all other conditions battle cannot be avoided without incurring dishonour and danger, for if you run away, as Philip did, it is as bad as being routed, and is the more shameful in that you afford less proof of your virtue. And if he thus succeeded in getting away, another who is not helped by the country may not be so successful as he was.

That Hannibal was a past master in warfare no one will deny. Hence, when he was up against Scipio in Africa, if he had seen any advantage in prolonging the war he would have done so; and peradventure, being a good general and having a good army, he might have done as Fabius did in Italy. But, as he did not do it, it must be supposed that strong grounds impelled him to act thus. For a commander who has an army massed together and sees that for lack of funds or of allies he cannot keep it long in the field, is quite mad if he does not put his fortune to the test before his army has to be disbanded; because, if he waits, he is surely lost; but if he tries, he may succeed.

Another point of importance to be considered here is that one ought, if one is going to lose, to try to acquire glory, and there is more glory in being overcome by force than there is when it is through some other inconvenience that you come to lose. Hannibal must have been constrained by these necessities. On the other hand, should Hannibal have put off giving battle and Scipio had not enough courage to go and attack him in his strong positions, Scipio would have been none the worse for this, since he had already beaten Syphax and acquired so many towns in Africa that his position there was as safe and as comfortable as if he were in Italy. This was not the case with Hannibal when he was up against Fabius, nor with the Gauls when they were up against Sulpicius.

Still less, again, is it possible for him to avoid battle who with his army is attacking a foreign country, for if he wants to get into the enemy's country, it behoves him when the enemy shows fight, to give battle, and if he takes up his position before a town, he is so much the more obliged to give battle. This happened in our times in the case of Charles, Duke of Burgundy, who, when encamped before Morat, a Swiss town, was attacked and routed by the Swiss; and in the case of the French army which was besieging Novara and was in like manner routed by the Swiss.

> *That he who has to deal with several Foes,*
> *even though he be Weaker than they are,*
> *can actually Win, provided he can sustain*
> *their First Attack*

The power of the tribunes of the plebs in the city of Rome was considerable, which was necessary since otherwise they could not have checked the ambition of the nobility, as we have frequently pointed out; and the nobility would in that case have corrupted the republic long before they did. Nevertheless, because inherent in everything is its own peculiar malady, as has been said elsewhere, and this gives rise to fresh misfortunes, it is necessary to provide against them by fresh enactments. Hence, when the tribunes grew arrogant in the use of their authority and became a menace alike to the nobility and to the whole of Rome, there would have arisen an inconvenience harmful to Roman liberty if Appius Claudius had not shown how the ambition of the tribunes might be counteracted. This consisted in looking among them for someone who was either timorous or corruptible or devoted to the common good, and who could thus be induced to oppose the will of the rest when they were proposing to do something contrary to the will of the senate. This remedy acted in no small measure as a restraint on the excessive authority of the tribunes and was often of service to Rome.

This leads me on to consider how it sometimes happens that, when many powers are united against a single power, though in combination they are much more powerful than it is, yet more is always to be expected from the single power, though less strong, than from the many even though very strong, for apart from the many advantages which a single power has over the many – and they are countless – there is always this: it will be able by using a little industry to break up the many, and to make what was a strong body, weak. I shall not adduce examples from ancient history, for they would be many, but shall content myself with modern examples which have happened in our own times.

In 1483 all Italy formed a confederation against the Venetians, who, since they had lost everything and their army could no longer hold its own in the field, suborned Signor Ludovico who was ruling in Milan and by means of this managed to obtain terms by which they not only recovered their lost lands, but obtained part of the state of Ferrara. Thus, though they were losing the war, when peace came, they were better off than before.

A few years ago the whole world formed a confederation against France, yet, before the war came to an end, Spain had fallen out with the confederation and made peace on its own account, with the result that the remaining confederates shortly afterwards also had to come to terms with France.

The conclusion to be drawn from this is obvious. If the many make war on the one, the one will come out of it best provided her virtue be such that she can sustain the first attack and await her opportunity by procrastinating. For, should she not be able to do this, a host of dangers may ensue, as happened to Venice in 08 when, could she have temporized with the French army and have found time to win over one of the states confederated against her, she might have avoided disaster. But since in arms she was not sufficiently strong to be able to temporize with the enemy, and so had not time to persuade any power to leave the confederation, she was undone. Yet one finds that the Pope, once he had recovered his lost territory, became her ally, and so did Spain; and either of these two princes would have been very glad to help her to save Lombardy so as to prevent the French becoming too powerful in Italy, had they been able to do so. Hence the Venetians, by giving up part of their territories, might have saved the rest; and this would have been a very wise course had it been done in time before the war broke out so that they should not appear to have been driven to it. But after the war had begun it would have been reprehensible, and probably of but little use. Yet, before war broke out, few Venetian citizens saw the danger, and still fewer the remedy; and there was no one to advise them.

But to come back to where we started. The conclusion I draw from this discourse is that, just as the Roman senate found means to save their country from the ambition of the tribunes because there were many tribunes, so any prince who is assailed by many, has a remedy to hand, if he be wise enough to take appropriate steps to break up the confederation.

That a Prudent General should make it absolutely necessary for his own Troops to Fight, but should avoid forcing the Enemy to do so

We have in other discourses shown how useful a part necessity plays in human affairs, and to what glorious deeds it may lead men. As some moral philosophers in their writings have remarked, neither of the two most noble instruments to which man's nobility is due, his hands and his tongue, would have attained such perfection in their work or have carried man's works to the height which one can see they have reached, if they had not been driven to it by necessity. Since, therefore, army commanders of old were aware of the virtue that lies in necessity, and how steadfast, when necessity drives, the minds of soldiers can become in their resolve to fight, they used every endeavour to put their troops under such constraint and, on the other hand, employed any device that would free the enemy from such constraint. To this end they often left open to the enemy a route they might have closed, and closed a route to their own soldiers which they might have left open. If, then, anyone wants a city to be obstinately defended or an army in the field to fight obstinately, he should, first and foremost, seek to instil this necessity into the minds of those who have to do the fighting.

It follows that a prudent general who has to go and lay siege to a city should base his estimate of how easy or how difficult it is going to be to take it on the knowledge and consideration of the extent to which necessity will constrain the inhabitants to defend it; and, if he find the necessity constraining them to defend it, considerable, should account the siege difficult, but, if otherwise, should account it easy. It is for this reason that towns which have rebelled are more difficult to acquire than they are to acquire in the first instance; for in the first instance they have no cause to expect punishment for having given offence, and so surrender easily; but, since they are aware, when in revolt, of having given offence, and in consequence fear punishment, they become difficult to take. Again, obstinacy of this kind is also aroused by the natural hatred which neighbouring princes and neighbouring republics have for one another; which, in turn, is occasioned by the ambition which moves states to dominate one another, and by their jealousy, especially if they are republics, as was the case in Tuscany, and this rivalry and competition have made it difficult, and will continue to make it difficult, for one to seize the other. If, therefore, one considers carefully what neighbours the city of Florence has and what neighbours the city of Venice has, it is not so extraordinary as many make out that Florence should have spent more on wars and have acquired less than Venice, since it is all due to the towns in the neighbourhood of Venice not being so obstinate in defending themselves as are those in the neighbourhood of Florence. This comes about because the cities abutting on Venetian territory are accustomed to live under a prince, and are not free cities; and cities accustomed to subjection are usually not so particular about changing masters: on the contrary, they are often glad to do so. Hence, though Venice's neighbours are more powerful than those of Florence, yet, on account of its having found the towns less obstinate, Venice has been able to subdue them more quickly than has Florence, which is surrounded entirely by free cities.

But to return to the main topic of this discourse. When a general is attacking a town he should endeavour with all diligence to relieve its defenders of the necessity we have been discussing, and so of their obstinacy; by promising them pardon if they are afraid of punishment, and, if they fear for their liberty, by explaining that no attack is being made on the common good, but only on a few ambitious citizens. This has often facilitated the attack on, and the taking of, towns. And, though such false colours are easily seen through, especially by men of prudence, the populace is none the less often deceived; for, in its eagerness for a speedy peace it shuts its eyes to any trap which may underlie generous promises. Innumerable cities have by this means been reduced to servile states. It was so with Florence, for instance, quite recently; and it happened to Crassus and his army; for, though he realized the emptiness of Parthian promises, made merely to deprive his troops of the need to defend themselves, this did not enable him to sustain their steadfastness, blinded as they were, by the offers of peace which the enemy had made: a point one sees clearly if one reads his life.

In this connection I might mention that when the Samnites, in contravention of their treaty and owing to the ambition of the few, raided and pillaged the lands of Rome's allies; and then sent ambassadors to Rome to sue for peace, offering to restore what they had taken and to hand over those responsible for the disturbances and for the booty taken, their offer was turned down by the Romans. On their returning to Samnium without hope of an agreement, Claudius Pontius, then in command of the Samnite army, in one of his remarkable speeches, pointed out that the Romans had anyhow wanted war, and that, though on their part they were anxious for peace, necessity constrained them to go to war. He then used these words: 'War is justified, if necessity forces one to it, and to arm is a duty, if in arms lies one's hope' and upon this necessity he based the hope of victory for his troops.

That I may not have to return later to this topic, it will be best for me to mention the more noteworthy instances in Rome's case. There was that of Gaius Manlius who led his army against the Veientes, and, when a section of the Veientine army broke through his stockades, hurried with a detachment to defend them and, to prevent the Veientes escaping, put a guard on all the exits from the camp. Hence, finding themselves shut in, the Veientes began to fight so furiously that they killed Manlius, and would have got the better of all the rest of the Romans if one of the tribunes had not had the sense to let them out. Thus we see that, so long as necessity constrained the Veientes to fight, they fought with great ferocity, but, when they saw the way was open, thought more of getting away than of fighting.

The armies of the Volsci and the Aequi had crossed the Roman frontiers. Against them the consuls were sent. In the course of the battle the Volscian army, commanded by Vettius Messius, found itself at one moment shut up between its stockades which the Romans had taken, and the other Roman army. Seeing that he must needs die or use his sword to fight for his life, Vettius Messius said to his soldiers: 'Follow me. There is neither wall nor rampart in the way, but just armed forces to oppose armed forces. In valour we are equal, but in necessity which is the last weapon and the best of all, you have the advantage.' Thus Livy calls necessity 'the last and best of all weapons'.

Camillus, the most prudent of all Rome's generals, having already got into the city of Veii with his army, in order to facilitate the taking of it and to deprive the enemy of a last necessity to defend it, gave orders within the hearing of the Veientes to the effect that no one should touch those who were without arms. The result was that they threw down their arms and the city was taken almost without bloodshed. This device was afterwards adopted by many generals.

Which is it best to trust, a Good General with a Weak Army or a Good Army with a Weak General?

Coriolanus, being banished from Rome, went to the Volsci, where, having got together an army wherewith to avenge himself on his fellow citizens, he set out for Rome, but turned back rather out of devotion to his mother than to the Roman forces. Commenting on this incident, Livy remarks that from it we may learn that the Roman republic grew more through the virtue of her generals than through that of her soldiers for, in view of the fact that the Volsci had thus far always been beaten, they could have won on this occasion only because Coriolanus was their general. But, though Livy advances this opinion, many passages in his history show that soldiers without a general have given remarkable proof of their virtue, and that they have been better disciplined and more determined after the death of their consuls than before they got killed. It happened thus with the army the Romans had in Spain under the Scipios, for, when both these generals had been killed, its virtue was such that not only did it successfully defend itself, but it beat the enemy and thus saved this province for the republic. Hence all things considered, there are many cases in which the virtue of the soldiers alone has won the day, and many others in which the virtue of generals has had the same effect, so that one can say that each has need of the other.

In this connection it will be well to consider first which is more to be feared: a good army badly generalled, or a good general who has poor troops. If we follow here the opinion of Caesar, neither one nor the other is worth much. For when he went to Spain against Afranius and Petreius, who had a first-class army, he showed how little esteem he had for them by remarking that 'he was going to fight an army without a general', thereby indicating the weakness of the generals. On the other hand, when he went to Thessaly to fight Pompey, he said: 'I am going to meet a general without an army'.

We can now turn to the further question: whether it is easier for a good general to make a good army, or for a good army to make a good general. I submit that on this point there can be no dispute; for it is easier for many, if good, to select or make a good man of someone, than it is for one good man to do it for many. Lucullus, when he was sent against Mithridates, was wholly without experience of warfare; yet the army, which was good and had excellent officers, soon made him a good general. Again, the Romans, who were short of men, armed a number of slaves, and handed them over to Sempronius Gracchus to train, and in a short time he made of them a good army. Pelopidas and Epaminondas, as I have remarked elsewhere, when they had delivered Thebes, their fatherland, from servitude to the Spartans, in a short time made such excellent soldiers of the Theban peasants that they could not only stand up against the Spartan militia but beat it.

The arguments are evenly balanced, because, if one is good, it can make the other like it. A good army, none the less, if it lacks a good head is apt to become mutinous and dangerous, as happened with the Macedonian army after the death of Alexander, and with the veterans in the civil war. Hence I am of opinion that more confidence should be placed in a good general who has time to train his men and a chance to arm them, than in a mutinous army with a turbulent fellow it has chosen as its head. Twice the glory and praise is due, then, to those generals who have not only had an enemy to beat, but, before coming to grips with him, have had to drill their troops and make a good army of them; for in this they display a twofold virtue, which is so rare that if it were given to many to be such strict disciplinarians, they would be much less esteemed and lauded than they are.

What Effects are produced by the Appearance of New Inventions in the course of a Battle and by the hearing of Unfamiliar Cries

Of what importance in strife and battle may be an unprecedented incident due to something seen or heard for the first time can be shown by numerous incidents and especially by that which occurred during the battle the Romans fought with the Volsci, when Quintius, seeing that one wing of his army was giving way, began to call to it in a loud voice to stand firm since the other wing was winning; for by these words he put courage into his own men and alarmed the enemy, and so won the day. And if on a well-disciplined army such remarks have a great effect, on a disorderly and ill-disciplined army they have a still greater effect, for the whole is swayed, as it were, by a wind.

Let me give you a remarkable instance which occurred in our own times. A few years ago, the city of Perugia was divided between two factions, the Oddi and the Baglioni. The latter were in power, the former having been banished. But, with the help of their friends, they got together an army and assembled it in one of their towns close to

Perugia. Then, with the connivance of their partisans they got one night into the city and were on their way to take the piazza without having been discovered. Since at every street corner in the city chains had been placed to block the way, the troops of the Oddi put at their head a man with an iron mace to break the locks fastening the chains so that the cavalry could get through. It remained for him to break only that which barred the way into the piazza when the cry 'To arms!' was raised, and on the fellow who was doing the breaking the crowd pressed so hard that he could not raise his arm to strike, so, in order to manage it, he called out 'Get back there!', words which, as they passed from rank to rank, became 'Get back!'. Whereupon those in the rear began to run away, and one after another, the rest followed suit with such frenzy that their own men were thrown into confusion. So that the plans of the Oddi came to nought owing to this insignificant incident.

This leads me to observe that good discipline is needed in an army not merely to enable it to fight in orderly fashion, but also that you may not be perturbed should some tiny misadventure befall. For this reason alone the masses are useless in war, since any rumour, any cry, any commotion may change their mood and make them run away. Hence it is essential to discipline that a good general should depute men to take note of his verbal instructions and to pass them on to others; that he should accustom his troops to pay no heed to anyone else, and his officers not to depart from what they have been commissioned by him to say; for we find that failure to observe these points carefully has often led to the greatest confusion.

In regard to strange sights, every general should try to present something of the sort while his army is in action so as to give courage to his own men and to dispel that of the enemy; for among the events which are incidental to victory this is especially effective. In illustration of this the case of Gaius Sulpicius, the Roman dictator, may be adduced, who, when engaged in battle with the Gauls, armed all his baggage-men and a low lot of camp-followers, put them on mules and other mounts so that with their arms and standards they looked like a troop of horse, and stationed them with flags flying behind a hill, with orders that, at a given signal when the fighting grew hotter, they should appear and show themselves to the enemy. This being done, as arranged, it so terrified the Gauls that they lost the day. There are two things, then, that a good general should do: first, he should see whether by employing some such novel device he can scare the enemy; and, secondly, he should be on the look-out so that, should the same trick be played on him by the enemy, he may discover it and nullify its effect.

It was thus that the King of India acted when Semiramis, noticing that the king had a good number of elephants, in the hope of intimidating him and showing him that she, too, had plenty of them, constructed a number of them out of the hides of buffaloes and cows and put them on camels which she sent ahead; but, the trick having been discovered by the king, her plan not only proved useless but turned out to her disadvantage. So, too, when the dictator Mamercus was at war with the Fidenates, to frighten the Roman army they ordered that in the heat of battle a number of troops should sally forth from Fidenae with torches on their lances in the hope that, distracted by the novelty of the thing, the Romans would break their ranks.

It should be noted here that, when such devices involve more truth than fiction, they can in that case be used on men with advantage, for if they have sufficient boldness, their weakness cannot be discovered so quickly. But when they involve more fiction than truth it is well either not to use them at all, or, if employed, to hold the performance some way off so that the fraud cannot be so quickly detected, as Gaius Sulpicius did with his muleteers. For if fraught with internal weakness, and they be near, they will soon be seen through, and will do you harm instead of good; as the elephants did to Semiramis and the torches to the Fidenates; for, though at the start they upset the army a little, yet, when the dictator came along and began to shout at the men, telling them not to be such cowards as to run away from the smoke like bees but to turn back and go for them, crying: 'Use the flames to destroy Fidenae since you have failed to pacify them with kindness', the device proved of no avail to the Fidenates, who were left the losers of the battle.

That at the Head of an Army there should be One, not Several, Commanders, and that to have a Plurality is a Nuisance

When the Fidenates rebelled and put to the sword the colony the Romans had sent to Fidenae, to right the insult the Romans appointed four tribunes with consular power, of whom one was left to guard Rome, and the other three were sent against the Fidenates and the Veientes. Owing to the divided command and to the tribunes being at loggerheads one with the other, they returned discredited, though there had been no disaster. For the discredit they were responsible, but that there had been no disaster was due to the valour of the troops. Hence when the Romans saw what was wrong, they had recourse to the appointment of a dictator so that one man should be responsible for putting right the disorder that three had caused. This shows us the futility of having several persons in command of the same army or in charge of the defence of the same town. Nor can the case be put more clearly than it is by Titus Livy when he writes: 'The three tribunes with consular power afforded an illustration of how futile it is for many to share the imperium in a war, for each inclined to follow his own counsel, and since the others thought otherwise, they gave the enemy their chance.'

And though this example is sufficient to show the disorders that a plurality of commanders causes in a war, I propose to give two more, one modern and the other ancient, the better to establish this point.

In 1500, after the King of France, Louis XII, had retaken Milan, he sent his troops to Pisa to recover it for the Florentines. The commissaries, Giovambatista Ridolfi and Luca di Antonio degli Albizi, were in command. Since Giovambatista was a man with a reputation and had seen more service, Luca left the management of everything to him, but though he did not display his own ambition by opposing him, he displayed it by his silence, by his negligence and by criticizing everything, with the result that he helped the siege operations neither by action nor advice, but behaved like a man of no account. Later on, however, when something occurred which necessitated Giovambatista's returning to Florence, one finds everything quite different; for, when Luca was left in sole charge, he showed his worth alike by his courage, his industry and his sound sense, all of which characteristics had failed to show themselves so long as he had a colleague.

In confirmation of this remark of Titus Livy's I would cite another example: the expedition which the Romans sent against the Aequi under Quintius and his colleague, Agrippa. Agrippa, who wanted the whole conduct of the war to be undertaken by Quintius, says: 'In the administration of affairs of moment it is highly advisable that the supreme command should be in the hands of one man'.

This is just the opposite of what our republics and princes do today, for to improve the administration they now send to a place more than one commissioner and more than one head, and this leads to indescribable confusion. Indeed, were one to seek the causes of the disasters that have befallen Italian and French armies in our own times, it would be found that this is the most potent. In conclusion, then, one may be quite certain that it is better to entrust an expedition to one man of average prudence than to give to two men of outstanding ability the same authority.

Advice to generals in the field

Reasons why the French have been, and still are, looked upon in the Beginning of a Battle as more than Men, and afterwards as less than Women

The ardour of the Gaul who challenged any Roman on the banks of the river Anio to single combat, which led to a fight between him and Titus Manlius, reminds me of what Titus Livy several times says of the Gauls, namely, that in the beginning of a battle they are more than men, but in the fighting that follows they turn out worse than women. As to how this comes about, many think that nature has made them so, which is no doubt true, but it does not follow from this that the nature which makes them ardent at the start could not be so regulated by rules as to keep them ardent right up to the end.

In proof of this let me point out that armies are of three types. In the first there is both ardour and order. Now order promotes both ardour and *virtù* as it did in the case of the Romans; for, during the whole course of their history one finds that there was good order in their armies, which military discipline of long standing had introduced. In a well-disciplined army, no one should perform any action except in accordance with regulations. Hence in the Roman army – which, since it conquered the world, should be taken as a model by all other armies – we find that no one ate or slept or went wenching or performed any other action, military or domestic, without instructions from the consul. Armies which act otherwise are not true armies; and if they do anything of note they do it through ardour and impetuosity, not through valour. But when disciplined *virtù* uses its ardour in the right way and at the right time, no difficulties dismay an army or cause it to lose courage. For good discipline stimulates courage and ardour, in that it strengthens the hope of victory, which is never wanting so long as discipline remains.

The opposite of all this happens in those armies in which there is ardour but no discipline, as was the case with the Gauls, who in their fighting were wholly lacking in method; for if their first attack did not succeed, they faltered, since the ardour on which they relied was not sustained by disciplined valour, and there was nothing else on which they could rely when their ardour cooled. The Romans, on the other hand, made light of dangers since their discipline was good; and, since they did not despair of victory, they remained firm and dogged, and fought with the same courage and the same *virtù* at the end as at the start; nay, when stimulated by a fight, they always grew more ardent.

The third type of army is one in which there exists neither a natural ardour, nor yet discipline to supplement it; as is the case with Italian armies in our day, which are quite useless and never win unless they come across an army which happens for some reason to run away. There is no need to cite further instances, since every day they afford evidence of how utterly lacking they are in valour. So that, however, what Titus Livy says may make it plain to all how good soldiery should be made and how worthless soldiery are made, I propose to cite the speech which Papirius Cursor made when he wanted to reprove Fabius, his master of horse. What he said was: 'No one would have respect either for men or for the gods; they would obey neither the edicts of generals nor the auspices; soldiers without provisions, would wander about here and there alike in peaceful and in hostile territory; forgetful of their oath, they would discharge themselves from the army without authority and when it pleased them; they would leave the colours almost unguarded, and neither assemble nor dismiss at the word of command; they would fight by day or night whether the place were suitable or unsuitable, and with or without orders from the general; they would keep neither to their regiments nor to their ranks; but, like a band of robbers, were a blind and tumultuous, rather than a disciplined and dutiful, soldiery.' And in this passage applied, it will at once be seen whether the soldiery of our day is blind and tumultuous or disciplined and dutiful, and how far it falls short of what we commonly call soldiery, and how far removed it is from being either ardent and disciplined, like the Romans, or just simply ardent, like the Gauls.

Whether Skirmishes are Necessary before a Battle, and how, if one decides to do without them, the Presence of Fresh Enemy Troops is to be discovered

It would appear that in human affairs, as we have remarked in other discourses, there is, in addition to others, this difficulty: that, when one wants to bring things to the pitch of perfection, one always finds that, bound up with what is good, there is some evil which is so easily brought about in doing good that it would seem to be impossible to have the one without the other. This is the case in everything that man does. And it is because of it that the good is with difficulty attained unless you are so aided by fortune that fortune itself eliminates this normal and natural inconvenience. What moves me to say this is the fight Manlius had with the Gauls, of which Titus Livy says: 'This conflict was of great moment to the outcome of the whole war, for the army of the Gauls in trepidation deserted their camp and moved first into Tiburtine territory, and then into Campania'; for I hold, on the one hand, that a good general ought to avoid at all costs doing anything which, though in itself of small moment, can produce a bad effect on his army; because to engage in a battle in which all one's forces are not employed and thereby to risk one's whole fortune, is extremely rash, as I said above when I was talking about guarding passes.

On the other hand, I hold that when wise generals find they are up against a new enemy who has acquired a reputation, it is essential that, before engaging in a pitched battle, they let their troops find out by means of skirmishes what he is worth; so that, having acquired some knowledge of him and of how to deal with him, it may dispel the fears to which rumour and his standing had given rise. For a general to do this is of the utmost importance; for there is in this course a quasi-necessity that constrains you to adopt it, since you can scarce fail to see that you are plainly exposing yourself to disaster if you engage the enemy without having first provided your troops with some little experiment whereby to rid them of that fear which the enemy's reputation had aroused in their minds.

Valerius Corvinus was in command of the armies which the Romans had dispatched to deal with the Samnites, new enemies, of whose fighting capacities the Romans had thus far had no experience in actual combat one with the other. Hence Titus Livy says that Valerius caused the Romans to engage in some skirmishes with the Samnites 'so that they might be afraid neither of the new war nor of the new enemy'. None the less, there is a very great danger that, if your soldiers get the worst of the skirmishing it will increase their fear and their cowardice, and so will produce the opposite effect to that you had in mind; i.e. you will have alarmed them, whereas you wanted to make them feel safe. So that this is just one of those things in which evil is so closely associated with good, and so bound up are they one with the other, that it may easily happen that he who thinks he will get one, gets the other.

In regard, then, to this, I maintain that a good general should take every precaution to prevent the occurrence of any untoward event likely to diminish the courage of his army. But to begin by losing is just the thing that is likely to diminish its courage. Hence he should act cautiously in regard to skirmishes, and should not permit them unless he has a great advantage and he feels sure he will be victorious. Nor should he attempt to guard passes where he cannot bring the whole of his army into operation. Nor yet should he defend towns unless their loss will inevitably entail his ruin. And, if he does defend them, he should arrange for his army to cooperate with the garrison in repelling an attack, so that in dealing with the siege all his forces may be brought into play; otherwise he should leave the town undefended. For in losing what may be abandoned, provided his army is still intact, he will not in such a case lose either his reputation in the war or the hope of winning it; but when you lose what you have planned to defend and everybody knows that you were defending it, the loss is serious and may be disastrous; in fact, you may, like the Gauls, on account of something of small moment have lost the war.

Philip of Macedon, the father of Perseus, a soldier of high standing in his day, when attacked by the Romans, abandoned and laid waste a large part of his country which he judged it impossible to defend, for, being a prudent man, he thought it more disastrous to lose his reputation by failing to defend what he had set out to defend, than to let it fall into the hands of the enemy as if it were a thing he did not mind losing. When after the defeat at Cannae the affairs of the Romans were in a bad way, they declined to help many of their dependents and subjects, bidding them defend themselves as best they could. Such courses are much better than taking up the defence of allies and then letting them down, for in that case one loses both one's allies and one's forces; but in the other the allies alone are lost.

But to return to skirmishing, I maintain that if a general is absolutely compelled to have recourse to skirmishes because his enemy is a new one, he should only undertake them when he has so considerable an advantage that there will be no danger of his losing thereby. He should, otherwise – and it is the better course – do as

Marius did when he went to fight the Cimbri, a fierce tribe which had come to prey upon Italy and which he was approaching with considerable trepidation owing to their ferocity and their numbers, and because they had already defeated a Roman army. Judging it necessary before engaging in battle to do something which would dispel the panic into which fear of the enemy had thrown his army, like a prudent general, he more than once stationed his army in a position near to which the army of the Cimbri must pass, with the intention that from behind the fortifications of their camp, his troops should look at and accustom their eyes to the enemy's appearance, so that when they saw what a disorderly crowd they were, encumbered with baggage, their arms useless and some without arms, they might be reassured and become eager for the fight. This course so wisely adopted by Marius, others should diligently imitate, so as not to incur the dangers I have described above, and not to have to act as the Gauls did, 'who, in trepidation on account of an event of small moment, moved first into Tiburtine territory and then into Campania'.

Since we have in this discourse mentioned Valerius Corvinus, I propose in the next chapter to use his speech to show how a general should behave.

What ought to be done by a General so that his Army may have Confidence in him

Valerius Corvinus, as we have said above, had gone with the army to fight the Samnites, enemies new to the

Roman people; so, to give his troops assurance and some acquaintance with the foe, he caused them to make a few skirmishes, and, since this was not enough, he decided to address them before the battle, and to point out as forcefully as he could how little esteem they should have for such a foe, appealing in his speech alike to the valour of his soldiers and to his own. From the speech which Livy makes him deliver, one may learn how a general should act if his army is to have confidence in him. What he says is this: 'Look at the man under whose leadership and auspices you are going to fight! Ask yourselves whether the person to whom you are about to listen is but a brilliant orator, valiant in words, but inexperienced in military matters, or whether he knows how to handle weapons, to advance before the colours, and to plunge right into the thick of the fight! I want you, my good men, to go by my actions, not my words, and to look to me not merely for orders, but for an example, for with this my right hand I have as a consul thrice won the highest praise.' Anyone may learn from a speech such as this, if he ponder it well, how to act if he wants to occupy the rank of a general; and he who acts otherwise will find that his rank, whether it be by luck or by ambition that he has attained it, in due course will destroy, instead of making, his reputation; for it is not titles that make men illustrious, but men who make titles illustrious.

One ought again in what was said at the outset of this discourse to observe that if great generals have used extraordinary means to strengthen the courage of a veteran army when confronted with an enemy with which it is unfamiliar, much greater industry will have to be used when in command of a new army which has never been in sight of the enemy. For if an enemy with which an old army is unfamiliar fills it with terror, so much the more must this be the case when a new army faces any enemy at all. Actually, however, one finds that all these difficulties are usually overcome by good generals with consummate prudence, as they were overcome by Gracchus the Roman, and by Epaminondas the Theban, of whom we have spoken on other occasions, for with new armies they defeated veteran armies with plenty of experience.

The methods they adopted were to exercise the troops for several months and to accustom them to obey orders by means of sham fights, after which they had so much confidence in them that they took them to a real fight. No military man, therefore, should be diffident as to his ability to form a good army, when there is no lack of men; so that the prince who has an abundance of men, but lacks soldiers, should bewail not the cowardice of his men, but merely his own laziness and folly.

That a General ought to be acquainted with the Lie of the Land

Among other things essential to the commander of an army is a knowledge of terrains and of countries, for, unless he has this knowledge, alike general and detailed, no army commander can perform any operation well. Wherefore, just as all sciences demand practice if we desire to attain perfection in them, so this is one that calls for a good deal of practice. And this practice and this detailed knowledge are acquired more by hunting, than by any other exercises. Hence ancient writers tell us that the heroes who ruled the world in their day were brought up in the forests and on the chase. For the chase not only provides one with the requisite knowledge, but teaches one a host of other things that are essential in warfare. Thus, Xenophon in his *Life of Cyrus* tells us how, when he was about to attack the king of Armenia, in appointing tasks he reminded those about him that it would be just like one of those hunting expeditions on which they had often accompanied him; and to those whom he sent to form an ambush in the mountains he said that they would be like men going to lay snares on the ridges; and to those who had to scour the countryside that they would be like men who went to rouse a wild beast from its lair so as, after hunting it, to drive it into the nets.

This I mention to show that Xenophon supports the view that a hunting expedition is very like a war, and that, consequently, great men look on this sport as honourable and necessary. Nor yet can a knowledge of the country be acquired in a more convenient way than by hunting, for the chase gives those who engage in it an exact knowledge of the lie of the land in which the sport takes place. It also enables one who has familiarized himself with one district, to grasp with ease the details of any new region. For all countries and all their parts have about them a certain uniformity, so that from the knowledge of one it is easy to pass to the knowledge of another; whereas he who has not acquired a good experience of any one can with difficulty acquire a knowledge of another, and cannot acquire it at all unless he is there for a long time.

A person who has had practice, for instance, will see at a glance how far this plain extends, to what height that mountain rises, where this valley goes, and everything else of this kind, for of it all he has already acquired a sound knowledge.

That this is so Titus Livy shows us in the case of Publius Decius. When he was a tribune in charge of troops belonging to the army which the consul, Cornelius, commanded in the Samnite war, and the consul had led the Roman army into a valley where it could have been shut in by the Samnites, Decius saw the great danger to which it was exposed, and said to the consul: 'Do you see, Aulus Cornelius, that peak above the enemy? It is in that height that lies our hope of safety if we take it quickly, the Samnites having stupidly neglected it.' Also, before telling us what Decius said, Titus Livy says: 'Publius Decius, a military tribune, observed a hill which rose above a wooded ravine and threatened the enemy's position, difficult of access to an army in marching order, but not difficult to light troops.' Whereupon he was sent there by the consul with three thousand soldiers and so saved the Roman army. Then, when night came on, and he was thinking of departing so as to save both himself and his troops, Livy makes him use these words: 'Come with me while the light holds, and let us reconnoitre the places in which the enemy has placed guards to see whether there is any way out'. All of which he carried out clad in a small military cloak, lest the enemy should notice an officer wandering about.

This evidence all goes to show how useful and necessary it is for a general to know the nature of the country;

for, if Decius had not been a prudent man and acquired such knowledge, he would not have been able to see how useful it was to the Roman army to take that hill, nor would he have been able to tell from a distance whether the hill was accessible or not; nor yet, when he had been sent to the top of it and wanted to get back to the consul, would he, with the enemy on all sides, have been able to spot from a distance the way to go and the places which the enemy was guarding. One is bound then to infer that Decius had such expert knowledge, and that it was this that enabled him to save the Roman army by taking the hill, and afterwards when he was surrounded there, to discover a route whereby both he and the troops that were with him could reach safety.

Salus populi, suprema lex

That it is a Glorious Thing to use Fraud in the Conduct of a War

Although to use fraud in any action is detestable, yet in the conduct of a war it is praiseworthy and glorious. And a man who uses fraud to overcome his enemy is praised, just as much as is he who overcomes his enemy by force. This is seen in the judgement pronounced on great men by biographers, who praise Hannibal and others well known for this kind of behaviour. Of this one comes across so many examples that I shall not cite any, I will say but this, I do not mean that a fraud which involves breaking your word or the contracts you have made is glorious; for, although on occasion it may win for you a state or a kingdom, as has been said in an earlier discourse, it will never bring you glory. I am speaking of fraud used in dealing with an enemy who has not kept faith with you, i.e. of the fraud which is involved in the conduct of a war; such as that which Hannibal used when at the Perugian lake he pretended flight in order to entrap the consul and the Roman army, and when, to escape from the hands of Fabius Maximus he lit up the horns of a herd of cattle.

To this class of fraud belongs that which was practised by Pontius, the general of the Samnites, that he might entrap the Roman army in the Caudine Forks. Having placed his army up against the mountains, he sent some of his soldiers, dressed as shepherds, with a flock of sheep across the plain. They were captured by the Romans, who asked where the Samnite army was. All agreed in saying what Pontius had told them to say, i.e. that it had gone to lay siege to Nocera. The credence given by the consuls to this report led to their being caught between the Caudine cliffs, where, when they got there, they were at once hemmed in by the Samnites. This victory, which Pontius gained by fraud, would have redounded greatly to his credit had he followed his father's advice, which was that he should either let the Romans go scot-free or should slaughter them all, and that he should not take the middle course which 'neither makes you friends, nor removes your enemies'; and this middle course has always been harmful in affairs of state, as I have already pointed out in another discourse.

That one's Country should be defended
whether it entail Ignominy or Glory,
and that it is Good to defend it in
any Way Whatsoever

The consul and the Roman army were surrounded by the Samnites, as has just been said. The Samnites had imposed on the Romans ignominious conditions. They were to pass under the yoke and to be sent back to Rome without their arms and equipment. At this the consuls, being astonished and the whole army being in despair, Lucius

Lentulus, the Roman legate, told them that it did not seem to him that they should reject any alternative in order to save their country; for, since the survival of Rome depended on the survival of this very army, it should be saved in any way that offered; and that it is good to defend one's country in whatever way it be done, whether it entail ignominy or glory; for, if this army was saved, Rome might in time wipe out the ignominy; but that, if it were not saved and even if it should die gloriously, Rome and its freedom would be lost. So Lentulus's advice was followed.

This counsel merits the attention of, and ought to be observed by, every citizen who has to give advice to his country. For when the safety of one's country wholly depends on the decision to be taken, no attention should be paid either to justice or injustice, to kindness or cruelty, or to its being praiseworthy or ignominious. On the contrary, every other consideration being set aside, that alternative should be wholeheartedly adopted which will save the life and preserve the freedom of one's country.

This is the course the French adopt – both in what they say and what they do – in order to defend the majesty of their king or the power of their kingdom; for no voice is heard with greater impatience than one that should say: 'Such an alternative it would be ignominious for the king to adopt.' No decision the king makes can be shameful, they say, whether it leads to good or to adverse fortune, for, whether he wins or loses is entirely his business, they claim.

That Promises extracted by Force ought not to be kept

When with an army that had been stripped of its arms and had suffered such ignominious treatment, the consuls returned to Rome, the first person to speak in the senate said that the peace made at Caudium ought not to be observed. This was the consul, Spurius Postumius. He said that the Roman people were not bound by it, but that he and the others who had promised peace were bound by it. Hence, if the people wanted to be free from any obligation, they should send him and all those who had made the promise back to the Samnites as prisoners. He defended this view with such tenacity that the senate yielded, sent him and the others as prisoners to Samnium, and protested to the Samnites that the peace was invalid. Fortune favoured Postumius in this case, for the Samnites did not keep him, and on his return to Rome he gained more glory in the eyes of the Romans by having surrendered than Pontius gained in the eyes of the Samnites by his victory.

Two things should here be noted. One is that glory can be gained by either kind of action, for it is acquired by victory in the ordinary course, and in defeat it is acquired if you can either show that the defeat was not your fault, or can at once perform some virtuous action which cancels it out. The other is that it is not shameful to fail to keep a promise which you have been forced to make. Forced promises affecting the public will, in fact, always be broken when the force in question is removed, and this without shame to those who break them. Everywhere in history one comes across examples of this of one kind or another, and everyone is aware that it happens also at the present day. And not only are forced promises not observed by princes when the force in question is no longer operative; but we also find that all other promises are broken when the reasons which caused such promises to be made no longer hold good. Whether this is praiseworthy or not, and whether a prince should or should not behave in this way, we have discussed at length in our treatise on *The Prince*. Here, therefore, nothing will be said about it.

THE STORY OF PENGUIN CLASSICS

Before 1946 ... 'Classics' are mainly the domain of academics and students; readable editions for everyone else are almost unheard of. This all changes when a little-known classicist, E. V. Rieu, presents Penguin founder Allen Lane with the translation of Homer's *Odyssey* that he has been working on in his spare time.

1946 Penguin Classics debuts with *The Odyssey*, which promptly sells three million copies. Suddenly, classics are no longer for the privileged few.

1950s Rieu, now series editor, turns to professional writers for the best modern, readable translations, including Dorothy L. Sayers's *Inferno* and Robert Graves's unexpurgated *Twelve Caesars*.

1960s The Classics are given the distinctive black covers that have remained a constant throughout the life of the series. Rieu retires in 1964, hailing the Penguin Classics list as 'the greatest educative force of the twentieth century.'

1970s A new generation of translators swells the Penguin Classics ranks, introducing readers of English to classics of world literature from more than twenty languages. The list grows to encompass more history, philosophy, science, religion and politics.

1980s The Penguin American Library launches with titles such as *Uncle Tom's Cabin*, and joins forces with Penguin Classics to provide the most comprehensive library of world literature available from any paperback publisher.

1990s The launch of Penguin Audiobooks brings the classics to a listening audience for the first time, and in 1999 the worldwide launch of the Penguin Classics website extends their reach to the global online community.

The 21st Century Penguin Classics are completely redesigned for the first time in nearly twenty years. This world-famous series now consists of more than 1300 titles, making the widest range of the best books ever written available to millions – and constantly redefining what makes a 'classic'.

The Odyssey continues ...

The best books ever written

PENGUIN 🐧 CLASSICS

SINCE 1946

Find out more at www.penguinclassics.com